SAILOR'S TERM	
Calm	
Light air	 appearance of scales
Light breeze	Small wavelets still short; crests have glassy appearance but do not break
Gentle breeze	Large wavelets; crests begin to break; scattered white horses
Moderate breeze	Small waves becoming longer; fairly frequent white horses
Fresh breeze	Moderate waves taking a more pronounced long form; many white horses; chance of spray
Strong breeze	Large waves begin to form; white foam crests more extensive; spray probable
Moderate gale	Sea heaps up and white foam from breaking waves begins to be blown in streaks along the direction of the wind; spindrift
Fresh gale	Moderately high waves of greater length; edges of crests break into spindrift; foam is blown in well-marked streaks along the direction of the wind
Strong gale	High waves; dense streaks of foam along the direction of the wind; sea begins to roll; spray affects visibility
Whole gale	Very high waves with long overhanging crests; resulting foam in great patches is blown in dense white streaks along the direction of the wind; the sea surface takes on a white appearance; rolling of the sea becomes heavy; visibility affected
Storm	Exceptionally high waves; small- and medium-sized ships may be lost to view behind the waves for a long time; sea is covered with long white patches of foam; everywhere the edges of the wave crests are blown into foam; visibility affected
Hurricane force	The air is filled with foam and spray; sea is completely white with driving spray; visibility very seriously affected

FAMOUS
IRISH
MARINERS

Emma Byrne is an award-winning graphic designer and artist. She has illustrated many books, including *Best-Loved Oscar Wilde*, *Best-Loved Yeats*, *The Most Beautiful Letter in the World* by Karl O'Neill, a special edition of *Ulysses* by James Joyce and *A Terrible Beauty* by Mairéad Ashe Fitzgerald. Her other books are *Irish Thatch* and, with Eoin O'Brien, *Best-Loved Irish Ballads*.

FAMOUS
IRISH
MARINERS

EMMA BYRNE

THE O'BRIEN PRESS
DUBLIN

First published 2025 by
The O'Brien Press Ltd,
12 Terenure Road East, Rathgar,
Dublin 6, D06 HD27, Ireland.
Tel: +353 1 4923333
E-mail: books@obrien.ie
Website: obrien.ie
The O'Brien Press is a member of Publishing Ireland.

ISBN: 978-1-78849-492-2

8 7 6 5 4 3 2 1
29 28 27 26 25

Printed and bound by Drukarnia Skleniarz, Poland.

The paper in this book is produced using pulp from managed forests.

To the best of our knowledge, this book complies in full with the requirements of the
General Product Safety Regulation (GPSR). For further information and help with
any safety queries, please contact us at productsafety@obrien.ie.

Published in

DUBLIN
UNESCO
City of Literature

Great Irish books
O'BRIEN
obrien.ie

DEDICATION

To Mogue and Brigid Byrne,
who fostered my love of the sea
from the earliest of days.

ACKNOWLEDGEMENTS

Many thanks to Joe Varley, President of the National Maritime Museum,
for reading this book, and to his colleagues Richard McCormick and
Fergus Plunkett: their help was invaluable in researching this book.
Thanks to Patrick Flood, whose maritime history primer was a great
source of inspiration.

I am grateful to all in the Arklow Heritage Museum, who were
unfailingly obliging; to Harry Bhachu in Alamy for his assistance, and to
Bernard Picton for his photograph of *Edwardsia Delapiae* on page 93.
My thanks, too, to all the team at The O'Brien Press: Ivan, Kunak, Ruth,
Brenda, Gabbie, Joana, Robbie, Emma and Rebekah; my wonderful
editor Paula Elmore, who steadied the ship through all waters; Eoin
O'Brien for his eagle-eyed proofreading; and Lir Mac Cárthaigh for his
technical assistance.

Thanks to Peter O'Dwyer, Helen Carr, Nicola Reddy and Síne Quinn,
who were all hugely supportive of this book.

TABLE

of

CONTENTS

MAPS

SOUTH AMERICA

NORTH ATLANTIC OCEAN

PANAMA

VENEZUELA

GUYANA

SURINAME

FRENCH GUIANA

BOGOTA

COLOMBIA

ECUADOR

QUITO

Amazon

LIMA

PERU

BRAZIL

BOLIVIA

BRASILIA

SÃO PAULO

PARAGUAY

SANTIAGO

CORRIENTES

Plata

URUGUAY

BUENOS AIRES

MONTEVIDEO

LA PLATA

ARGENTINA

CHILE

SOUTH PACIFIC OCEAN

SOUTH ATLANTIC OCEAN

FALKLAND ISLANDS

SOUTH GEORGIA
AND SOUTH SANDWICH ISLANDS

CANADIAN ARCTIC

GREENLAND

Wreck of
HMS *Investigator*

Melville Island

Cornwallis
Island

Baffin Bay

Banks Island

Cape Bathurst

Melville Sound

ARCTIC CIRCLE

NUNAVUT

Victoria Island

King William
Island

Baffin Island

Wreck of
HMS *Terror*

Wreck of
HMS *Erebus*

Melville
Peninsula

NORTHWEST TERRITORIES

CANADA

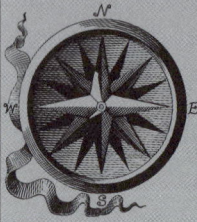

Hudson Bay

N

W

E

S

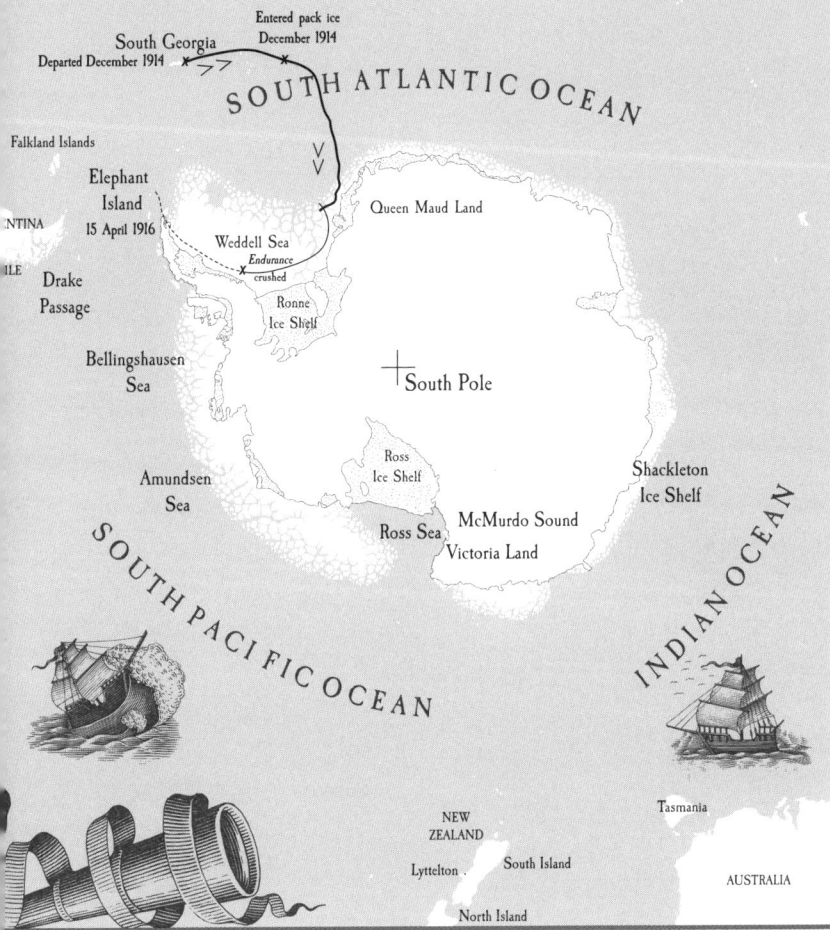

SOUTH
AFRICA

ANTARCTICA

Entered pack ice
December 1914

South Georgia

Departed December 1914

SOUTH ATLANTIC OCEAN

Falkland Islands

Elephant
Island

NTINA   15 April 1916

ILE   Drake
Passage

Queen Maud Land

Weddell Sea
Endurance
crushed

Ronne
Ice Shelf

Bellingshausen
Sea

+ South Pole

Amundsen
Sea

Ross
Ice Shelf

Shackleton
Ice Shelf

McMurdo Sound

Ross Sea

Victoria Land

SOUTH PACIFIC OCEAN

INDIAN OCEAN

Tasmania

NEW
ZEALAND

Lyttelton   South Island

AUSTRALIA

North Island

➤ *Endurance* route

CHRONOLOGY

INTRODUCTION

As an island nation, we Irish have a love and fascination for the sea. The first people in prehistoric times most likely came to Ireland by boat; since then we have sailed, fished, smuggled and fought our way through history and to every corner of the world, with the sea entwined in our DNA. It is a briny elixir that binds us.

The early missionary monks spread the word of the gospels here and abroad, making their voyages in currach-like vessels. We don't often think of them as accomplished sailors, but they must have had a great understanding of boats and the sea to make their journeys. The Brendan story is one mirrored by several sailor missionaries from this island: Colmcille left Derry for Iona in Scotland by sea in the middle of the sixth century, to establish an abbey there. Columbanus travelled from County Down to France and eventually to Bobbio in Northern Italy. He even composed a boating song for the crew as they rowed down the Rhine:

Lo, little bark
on the twin-horned Rhine,
From forest hewn,
to skim the brine.
Heave, lads, and let the echoes ring.

Dubhán, a missionary who came to Ireland from Wales around 452, established the first lighthouse, a fire signal, at Hook Head. He gave his name to the peninsula: originally Rinn Dubhán, or Dubhán's Point, his name also means 'fishing hook'. Aidan of Ferns became a disciple of David of Wales in the sixth century, and his journey also had to be made by sea.

The Vikings came to Ireland in longships from 795 and later, in the twelfth century, the Normans arrived in the southeast in similar vessels.

As conditions in Ireland were often harsh, many people left to seek their fortunes elsewhere, often fighting for foreign naval forces and often leaving at a very young age. As the great European empires – the Spanish, Portuguese and British – waned and nations claimed the right to self-rule, many opportunities arose for those who had the courage to embrace them. John Barry became known as the 'Father of the American Navy' and many others rose to national prominence in South America, as countries there freed themselves from Portuguese and Spanish rule.

As scientific discovery advanced in the nineteenth century, Irishmen such as Francis Beaufort would revolutionise navigation for seagoing vessels. Beaufort's work as Chief Hydrographer of the Royal Navy included standardising how weather conditions were described and also charting the seas. This not only made shipping safer, it also allowed for better planning of journeys. It was thanks to him that scientific investigation at sea became as important as the discovery of new lands.

The golden age of polar exploration saw many Irish involved at every level, and names such as Ernest Shackleton and Tom Crean are now embedded in the public consciousness.

In the twentieth century, the Allied sea commanders of both America and Britain were Irish: James Forrestal, United States Secretary of the Navy, was second-generation Irish and Andrew Cunningham, First Sea Lord of the British Admiralty, was born in Dublin.

There is no doubt that, for a small island nation on the very edge of Europe, we have punched above our weight when it comes to maritime achievement.

Like many of our island race, I have been fascinated by the sea from an early age. From peering into rock pools as a small child, to being in the sea scouts, to daily swimming and recreational scuba diving, I have spent as much of my free time as possible in the sea. The stories of these Irish mariners – some well known, some not so well known – were fascinating to research and I hope you'll enjoy reading about them.

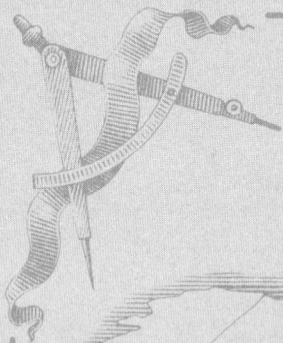

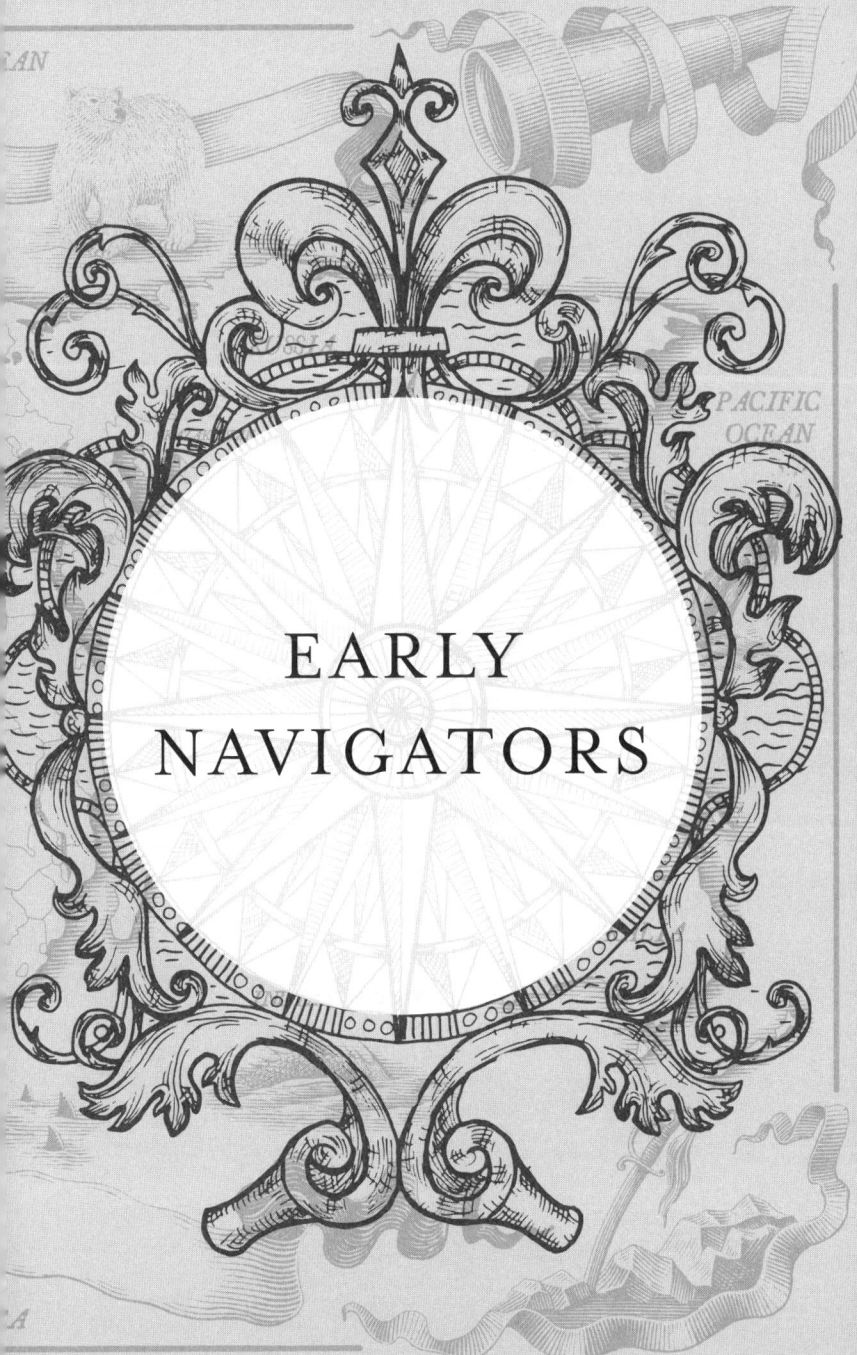

PACIFIC
OCEAN

EARLY
NAVIGATORS

A statue of St Brendan the Navigator in Wolfe Tone Square, Bantry, County Cork. Created by Ian and Imogen Stuart and unveiled in 1969, it faces the sea, just as Brendan did.

BRENDAN OF CLONFERT

484 – *c.* 577

Brendan of Clonfert – or Brendan the Navigator, as he was also known – was one of the early saints of Ireland who is reputed to have undertaken a heroic voyage in a skin boat to find his 'treasure island'. His story, a legend to Irish schoolchildren, comes from the old Irish tale of *Navigatio Sancti Brendani Abbatis* or *The Voyage of Saint Brendan the Abbot*.

*

The story of Brendan's life comes to us from the early Irish annals, and from Latin sources in other countries. He is mentioned as a seafarer in the *Martyrology of Tallaght*, a ninth-century list of saints and their feast days. Whilst details of his actual life and journey are scant, it shows that there was a devotion to him several centuries after his death.

It is thought that he was born in 484 in Tralee, County Kerry, into the Altraige clan. His parents were Finnlug and Cara. Brendan spent his early days in the Fenit area, and the windswept Tralee Bay, with its spectacular landscape and views out over the wild Atlantic, must have made a huge impression on the young boy. Between the ages of two and five, he was fostered and educated by St Ita in Killeedy, near Newcastle West in Limerick. He then returned to the Fenit area, to Ardfert, and was in the care of Bishop Erc, who taught him the Christian way of life. He was also taught by St Jarlath in Tuam and St Enda on Inishmore. All of this influenced Brendan's way of life, and his understanding and care of people, and to him ultimately following the tradition of the great early travelling monastic saints. He is thought of as one of the Twelve Apostles of Ireland.

Brendan was ordained as a priest by Bishop Erc when he was twenty-six. He then set off on his travels, founding several monasteries on islands off the Scottish coast near Argyll, where he met Colmcille. Brendan visited Iona, where Colmcille had established an important abbey. He also travelled to Wales and Brittany in northern France, where he met St Malo, himself a seafaring saint. An island in St Malo Bay, Cézembre, had a chapel dedicated to St Brendan (unfortunately destroyed by Allied bombing in 1944). Saint Brendan's Island, although mythical, appeared on maps from the period, including the Mappi Mundi, the great map of the world dating from 1300, and later on, the Erdapfel – 'world apple' or globe – of Martin Behaim from 1492.

The Irish missionary monks proved to be able seamen, and they navigated European and Atlantic waters to spread the word of God. In keeping with the monastic tradition of living lives of contemplation in isolated places, many of them found refuge on remote and windswept islands around Ireland. Early religious artefacts can be found on Dalkey Island, the Blaskets, the island of Tory with its Tau Cross and, famously, Skellig Michael with its distinctive beehive huts. To reach these places in often rough seas, it was necessary to have knowledge of the building and maintaining of boats as well as an understanding of tides and weather. Colmcille travelled to Scotland, as already mentioned, famously establishing a monastery on Iona. Fergus from Waterford travelled to Salzburg, and Columbanus and Gall also undertook sea journeys. They probably travelled in something akin to a currach, a small, leather-skinned boat, propelled both by oars and a mainsail.

Monasteries were not just singular buildings for contemplation and prayer, but could be sizeable villages, accommodating a cultivated farm and a school. The farm fed the local community and the school educated them. There was also the valuable scriptorium, used for the production of manuscripts. It took a great deal of organisational ability to create such a community.

Brendan founded his community at Clonfert, County Galway, using the knowledge he had gained overseas. He also built monastic cells at Ardfert, County Kerry, at the foot of the mountain now known as Mount Brandon. It was from here that Brendan departed on his epic seven-year voyage.

The legendary journey is said to have happened between 512 and 530. As an established missionary, Brendan felt the calling to bring the good news of Christ's teachings to the wider world. His friend Barinthus, a fellow monk recently returned from a sea voyage, described a Land of Promise. Filled with curiosity and wonder, Brendan was determined to find it. From his earlier voyages, he had gained considerable skill in seafaring and boatbuilding and, armed with an intense faith, he feared little.

His boat was a currach made using iron tools. The ribs and frame were made of wood and were covered with tanned cowhide, pre-stretched over oak bark. The seams on the outside surface of the skin were sealed with animal fat, to waterproof them. It would have been a very durable and light vessel. In 1976, Tim Severin, a noted British sailor who later made his home in west Cork, recreated the boat using traditional materials and building methods, and undertook a journey, which he recounts in his book *The Brendan Voyage*. He departed from Fenit, County Kerry, and arrived in Newfoundland on 26 June 1977, showing that the journey could have been successfully completed and that Brendan and his monks may have been the first to discover the North American continent, almost 500 years before the Viking explorer Leif Erikson and almost 1,000 years before Columbus.

Brendan chose fourteen fellow monks for his voyage and they set out from the coast of Kerry. They took food for forty days at sea as well as extra supplies of skins and tools. Their vessel had a mast and a sail. Three others joined the crew, and these three did not return, as prophesied by Brendan.

For seven years, they travelled westwards, encountering various locations in their search for the Promised Land. One of the first places they came across was an uninhabited island, where the first of the last three monks to join the crew died.

They continued on their journey to the Island of Sheep (probably one of the Faroe Islands). After a short stay, they set sail again and landed on what they believed was an island, but when they lit a fire, they discovered they had landed on the back of a giant fish, called Jasconius. The 'island' moved, hurling the monks into the sea. Brendan rescued them and saw from a safe distance the island dipping and plunging into the sea, giving him to believe that they encountered a great Leviathan of the deep.

Brendan and his crew arrived at an island inhabited by thousands of birds, with one of which Brendan is said to have conversed. The bird told him that on Sundays they became human and sang songs of praise. The journey also took them to the Island of Ailbe, which was inhabited by a community of monks. Here they received a warm but silent welcome, as the men conversed only at choir. Ailbe and his followers washed Brendan and the crew's feet, and fed them, which must have been of great comfort to the weary travellers. Next, they came across a huge white and silver column, probably an iceberg, and no doubt treacherous to a skin boat. They also encountered the Island of Strong Men. It is here that the second of the extra monks died, while the third was dragged away by demons.

After travelling for seven years, sometimes visiting places repeatedly, including meeting the great Jasconius again, they finally arrived at the Promised Land for Saints. Here they were greeted by a young man, who praised their endeavours. They stayed a short while and then made the return trip to Ireland, where they received a wonderful welcome. Back at Clonfert, Brendan told the community of their incredible voyage. He also told them he would die soon, and it was in Annaghdown, Galway, where he had established a monastery for his sister Briga, that he passed away. He is buried in Clonfert. There are two reports of his death in the Annals of Ulster of 577 and 583.

Fact or fiction, the story of Brendan became part of folklore. His name appeared on ancient maps: Brendan Island is marked on a Portuguese map from 1474 by Toscanelli, and this map was used by Christopher Columbus. It is argued that Columbus learned from the *Navigatio* that the winds and currents would suit westbound travel from

Europe. (Interestingly, another Irishman, Patrick Maguire, was Columbus's navigator and he may have been the first European to set foot on American soil.) The story of Brendan is also told in the Dutch *De Reis van Sinte Brandaen* (*The Voyage of Saint Brendan*), which dates from the twelfth century.

Numerous places are named in his honour, including Mount Brandon, Brandon Hill and Brandon Head. In Sicily, Italy, there is a small church dedicated to Brendan, called *San Brandanu.* It is thought the interest in Brendan came to the area with the Normans.

St Brendan's feast day is celebrated on 16 May. He is the patron saint of boatmen, seafarers, travellers and whales. He is also the patron saint of the US Navy.

Tim Severin reinacting the voyage of Brendan the Navigator in 1976.

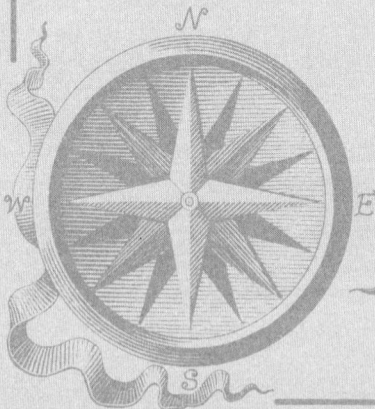

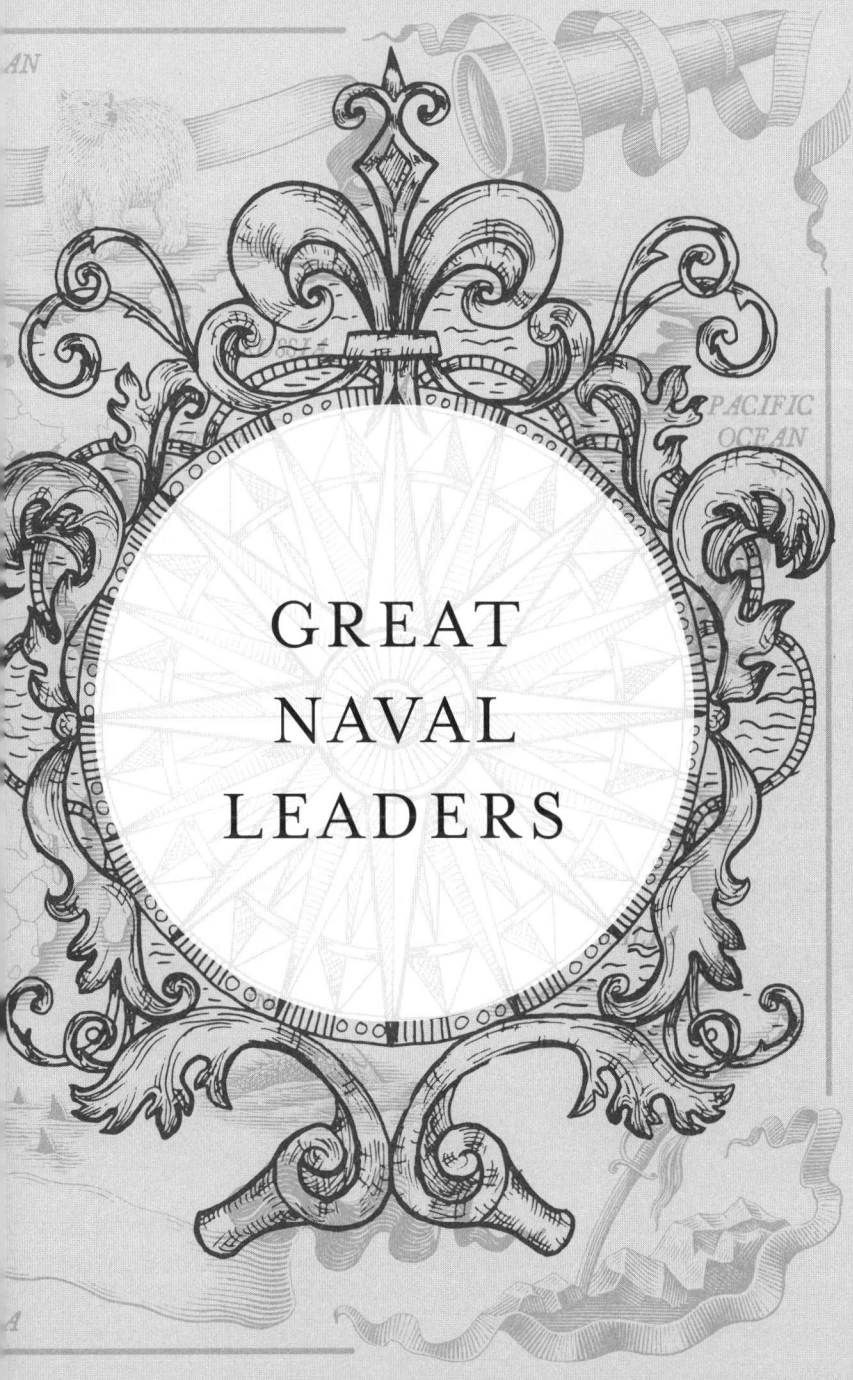

GREAT
NAVAL
LEADERS

A portrait of Commodore John Barry by Wilfred I. Duphiney (1884–1960).

JOHN BARRY

1745–1803

John Barry was the son of a poor Wexford farmer. He rose from his humble origins to become senior commander of the United States naval fleet. He well deserves the title 'Father of the American Navy'. The first to capture a British war vessel in the Revolutionary War, Barry captured another two British ships after suffering severe wounds in a sea battle; he quashed three mutinies, fought as a soldier in the Battles of Trenton and Princeton, captured over twenty ships and authored a signal book. He fought the last naval battle of the American Revolution aboard the frigate *Alliance* in 1783.

*

Born in Ballysampson, Tacumshane, County Wexford, on 25 March 1745, John Barry grew up in a Catholic family of tenant farmers. He was the eldest of James and Ellen Barry's six children. When the family were evicted in the mid-1750s by their English landlord, they moved to Rosslare, where John's uncle Nicholas Barry ran a fishing skiff. It must have set a light in the youngster, because he went to sea as a cabin boy at the age of nine. He next found a position as a seaman on a merchant vessel sailing between Europe and the Caribbean. He moved up the ranks from seaman to able seaman, eventually achieving a mate's rating.

In 1760, at the age of fifteen, he moved to Philadelphia in America and made the city his home. He went on to command several ships and became a hugely successful sea captain in the merchant shipping business.

His first command was in 1766 on the schooner *Barbadoes*, which sailed out of Philadelphia. The city was tolerant of Catholics and was emerging as an important maritime centre of trade. Its growing population required goods and therefore ships' captains to transport them, mainly between Philadelphia and the West Indies. This was the perfect schooling for a young man who was in command of several merchant ships. In trade with the West Indies, Barry made at least nine round trips without any mishaps.

Barry was making a name for himself in Philadelphia by now and had a strong reputation with many influential businesses in the city. He was employed by Robert Morris, the financier of the First Continental Congress in 1774. Morris was in partnership with two businessmen, Willing and Cadwalader, and Barry was assigned their 200-ton ship *Black Prince*. It was on board this vessel that Barry made the incredible record of travelling 237 nautical miles in a 24-hour period – the fastest day of sailing recorded in the eighteenth century.

This record-making voyage copper-fastened Barry's reputation. He returned to port in 1775 to discover that the colonies and Great Britain were at war. Barry offered his services to the rebel cause and joined the new American Continental Navy. Because of his reputation, he was given the task of outfitting the first Continental Navy ships, which were to sail from Philadelphia. His job was to make ready the ships, including rigging, creating gunports and procuring gunpowder and provisions. From this, he was rewarded with a captain's commission by the president of the Continental Congress, John Hancock, and given command of his first warship, the brigantine *Lexington*.

The *Lexington* went to battle with the British ship *Edward*, and made the first capture of a British warship by an American sailing vessel. Barry was only thirty-one.

Whilst waiting for his next command, the *Effingham*, to be completed, Barry served with a company of marines as aide-de-camp to General John Cadwalader, whose ship *Black Prince* he had captained. As a soldier, Barry distinguished himself in the Battle of Trenton (26 December 1776) and the Battle of Princeton (3 January 1777). General George Washington, Commander-in-Chief of the Continental Army and later the first US president, used Barry as a courier, bringing wounded prisoners through British lines.

In 1778, Barry attacked a British fleet with a flotilla

of small craft. With seven small boats, including barges, longboats and rowboats, he surprised and captured two armed sloops and a schooner. Other captured ships earned him a letter of commendation from General Washington.

Barry had a reputation for care of his crew at all costs, something best illustrated by what happened to the 32-gun frigate *Raleigh*. She was cornered in Maine's Penobscot Bay by two British ships, *Unicorn* and *Experiment*. Barry was unfamiliar with these northern waters and, hemmed in, he ran aground on Wooden Ball Island. Rather than let the British take his crew prisoner, he was determined to save them and set fire to the ship to prevent it falling into enemy hands. He succeeded in saving two-thirds of the crew, eighty-eight men, getting them to safety in rowboats to Boston. The British took the remaining third prisoner and managed to refloat the *Raleigh*, converting her to a Royal Navy vessel.

John Barry's best-known naval encounter was in command of the *Alliance*. She was a 36-gun frigate, the most popular ship in the Continental Navy owing to her excellent conditions, which consequently meant a contented crew. Off the coast of Newfoundland on 28 May 1781, the *Alliance* encountered two British sloops, *Atlanta* and *Trespassy*. Although the *Alliance* fired first, she lost the wind and was becalmed, unable to move, and was attacked fore and aft by the British ships. Barry defended strongly from the quarterdeck until he was hit in the left shoulder by a canister shot, a rather nasty mixture of broken nails and metal fragments. When Barry was brought below, his second in command, Lieutenant Hoystead Hacker, urged him to surrender. Barry disagreed and insisted on being brought back on deck. Luckily at this point, *Alliance* had wind in her sails once again, and Barry turned his fourteen 12lb cannon on his foes. Battered, the *Atlanta* and *Trespassy* both surrendered, striking their colours. The engagement resulted in the loss of two British ships, eleven dead and twenty-five wounded. The British captain, Edwards, survived. He came on deck to present his sword to Barry, who received it but handed it back to Edwards, saying, 'Sir. You have merited it, and your King ought to give you a better ship. Here is my cabin, at your service. Use it as your own.' In all, Barry captured over twenty enemy ships during the War of Independence.

After the war, Barry captained the merchant ship *Asia* and worked the routes to China and the Orient, bringing porcelain back to the citizens of Philadelphia.

The Continental Navy, disbanded after the War of Independence, was reborn as the Federal Navy. Secretary of War Henry Knox appointed Barry Senior Captain. On 22 February 1797, President Washington gave Barry the position of Commission Number One, in effect recognising him as the United States' first commissioned naval officer, a title of great honour. Barry supervised the construction of the Federal Navy's first frigates, including his own 44-gun frigate USS *United States*.

Barry commanded all American ships during the undeclared war with France (1798–1800) under the courtesy title of Commodore. From 1789 to 1801, he was head Squadron Commander of the United States Naval Station in the West Indies at Guadeloupe.

Barry's service to the new navy included authoring a signal book in 1780, establishing an effective system of communication between ships at sea. He trained a great number of men, many of whom became heroes in the war of 1812 with Great Britain over British violations of US maritime rights. This earned Barry the title 'Father of the Navy'.

His personal life was not without tragedy. In 1767, he got married in Philadelphia to Mary Cleary from Wexford, but she died in 1774 at the age of twenty-nine. Her husband was unfortunately at sea at the time. He was married again, to Sarah 'Sally' Keen Austin, in 1777. Barry's brother Patrick was lost at sea. Patrick was aboard the ship *Union*, which sailed from Bordeaux in 1778 and was never seen again.

Barry remained head of the navy until his death on 12 September 1803 from complications with asthma. He was buried with full military honours in Philadelphia's Old St Mary's Churchyard.

A bronze statue of John Barry on Crescent Quay, Wexford, presented to the people of Ireland by the USA. Created by American sculptor Wheeler Williams in 1955, it was brought to Ireland on board the USS *John R. Pierce* and unveiled in 1956.

A daguerreotype of Admiral William Brown from 1857.

WILLIAM BROWN

1777–1857

As South America broke away from its colonial masters – Mexico, Uruguay, Venezuela, Peru and Chile from Spain; and Brazil from Portugal – opportunities opened up to many, and Irishmen were at the helm of naval life in South America. One such man was William Brown, founder of the Argentine Navy. He was deeply involved in the country's War of Independence with Spain and is regarded as one its great naval commanders and a national hero. He was known in Spanish as Guillermo Brown or Almirante Brown.

*

William Brown was born in Foxford, County Mayo, on 22 June 1777. Some sources suggest that he was an illegitimate son of one of the Brownes, a County Mayo family with connections to the Altamont family of Westport House. Lord Altamont married the daughter of Richard Howe, who was First Lord of the Admiralty at the time. Howe carried considerable influence, enough to get William and his brother positions in the Royal Navy.

After a short spell in the navy, Brown transferred to the merchant navy. He married Elizabeth Chitty on 29 July 1809 in Kent. Elizabeth's family had trade connections with Argentina and, later that year, Brown left Britain to work the trade between Montevideo and Buenos Aires on the Rio de la Plata, an estuary between Uruguay and Argentina, aboard the ship *Belmond*. In 1810, he arrived at the port of Buenos Aires to find it blockaded by Spanish ships and thus became involved in the Argentine War of Independence.

Spanish ships destroyed Brown's own schooner and other trading vessels. The revolutionary junta seeking independence from Spain decided they had to protect their coast and shipping. They provided ships and appointed Brown as Commander-in-Chief of this fleet. During one incident, Brown's second in command, American-born Benjamin Franklin Seavers, died trying to break the Spanish blockade. Angered, Brown launched a full-scale attack on the Spanish with his fleet of seven poorly armed ships in early March 1814.

Despite losing his flagship *Hercules* when she ran aground, he eventually succeeded in taking possession of Martín García, a well-armed island some twenty miles from Buenos Aires. Control of it was key to the situation. Brown's forces were augmented to by three heavily armed Argentine merchant ships. The Spanish fleet was itself now cornered by Brown's fleet at Montevideo.

As the blockade continued, the city was threatened with starvation. The battle wore on, and at one stage a cannonball shattered Brown's leg, but he carried on issuing orders, undeterred. Eventually, three of the Spanish ships were captured, and Rio de la Plata was released from Spanish control, a great win for the newly independent Argentina.

After the battle, Brown continued to be a threat to the Spanish, harassing their ships not only around Argentina, but along the west coast of South America and in the Pacific.

In December 1825, war broke out between Argentina and Brazil. Uruguay, and the control of it, had always been a point of contention between Spain and Portugal, and that animosity now shifted to Argentina and Brazil. Brown was persuaded to come out of retirement to build and equip a fleet of ships. He won a number of major battles: in Montevideo, Pozos, Juncal, Quilmes, and Martín García. In October 1827, the Treaty of Montevideo was signed, a peace treaty that recognised the independence of Uruguay, with William Brown acting as the Argentine commissioner.

In 1828, Brown was appointed Governor of Buenos Aires and later led a successful campaign against Guiseppe Garibaldi in Uruguay. (The same Garibaldi later achieved great fame in unifying Italy.)

In 1847, Brown returned to visit Foxford with his daughter. Back in Argentina, he was honoured for his long service to the Argentine Navy. He died on 3 March 1857 and was buried with full military honours. He is buried in La Recoleta Cemetery in Buenos Aires.

Brown's legacy is considerable. He is commemorated on stamps both in Ireland and Argentina. Replicas of his sword are worn by admirals of the Argentine Navy. One resides in the National Maritime Museum of Ireland in Dún Laoghaire. The original sword is kept in the National Historical Museum of Argentina. There are memorials to Brown in Foxford, Dublin and Buenos Aires.

The Brownian National Institute for maritime studies was unveiled in 1948 in Buenos Aires. Several warships have been named after him, including the Almirante Brown class of destroyers: four MEKO 360H2 type military ships commissioned for the Argentine Navy between 1983 and 1984 after the Falklands War. All four are still in service: *Almirante Brown*, *La Argentina*, *Heroína* and *Sarandí*. The Almirante Brown Antarctic Base is also named in his honour.

In 2006, the Irish Navy ship LÉ *Eithne* travelled to Buenos Aires for a commemoration of Brown's death, and to bring back a statue of him, which is displayed at Sir John Rogerson's Quay in Dublin. Its inscription is in English and Spanish, and shows the high regard in which the Argentinian people still hold him.

Top: An 1825 miniature portrait of William Brown by Henry Hervè.
Bottom: The Argentinian destroyer ARA *Almirante Brown* leads a formation off the coast of Brazil in 2005.

Uruguayan Navy vessels in Montevideo.

PETER CAMPBELL

1780–1832

Irishman Peter Campbell found great fame as the founder of the Uruguayan Navy.

*

Peter Campbell was born in Tipperary in 1780. There is little record of his early years, though it seems likely that he served an apprenticeship as a tanner. Like many of his nationality before and after, he enlisted in the British Army, and found a home with the 71st Highland Regiment of Foot, a Scottish light infantry unit.

This regiment, along with others, saw action in Buenos Aires in 1806, serving under William Carr Beresford during the Anglo-Spanish War, which was fought intermittently between 1792 and 1808. As part of this war, Britain attempted to take control of Spain's Viceroyalty of the Río de la Plata (which comprised parts of modern-day Argentina, Uruguay, Paraguay and Bolivia) in 1806–07.

When British forces failed to gain ground from the Spanish, Campbell stayed and joined the local patriot ranks as a guerrilla leader, causing trouble for the Spanish both on land and on the Paraná River. In addition to the long knife he used in duelling, he carried a sabre and two pistols. He gained a reputation as a formidable fighter, serving under José Artigas, a political leader and soldier who became the father of Uruguayan independence.

During the Argentine War of Independence (1810–18), Campbell established a cavalry regiment of indigenous people called the Tapé. They were greatly feared because of their effectiveness both on horseback and as an infantry unit. They would charge the enemy at speed, then dismount and open fire.

In 1814, Campbell assembled a squadron of vessels on the Paraná River to fight for Artigas, and in 1818, he took command of a second squadron. In August that year, he was appointed first naval commander of the Uruguayan fleet, in effect becoming the founder of the Uruguayan Navy. The following month, he captured two ships carrying arms for the Paraguayan army.

After 1819, Campbell acted as the Deputy Governor of Corrientes province (part of modern-day Argentina) and continued to campaign successfully for the Uruguayan Navy. In a naval battle in Monteverde in 1820, Artigas and Campbell were defeated. Campbell was captured and led away to Paraguay in shackles. The Paraguayan dictator, Francia, spared his life, perhaps out of respect for his courage and bravery, and allowed him to live quietly in Ñeembucú, where he remained until he died in 1832.

There is some confusion about both the precise date and location of his death. When his remains were discovered in 1961, they were handed over to Uruguay and reinterred in Montevideo in May that year, a more honourable resting place for the founder of that country's navy.

In the National Navy of Uruguay, a medal is named in his honour: the Decorative Honour of Naval Merit Commander Peter Campbell. A ship, ROU *Comandante Pedro Campbell*, is also called after him. Originally a minesweeper, it was reconfigured as a supply ship for the General Artigas Base in Antarctica, a Uruguayan scientific research station.

A nineteenth-century engraving of the Battle of Quilmes.

BARTHOLOMEW
HAYDEN
1792–1857

Bartholomew Hayden was an Irishman who rose to prominence as a fighter in the Brazilian War of Independence and acquired the rank of Commodore in that country's new navy.

*

Hayden was born in County Tipperary on 22 February 1792, to John and Joanna Hayden. He joined the Royal Navy as a young man and served during the Napoleonic Wars with France. A midshipman for twelve years, from 1803 to 1815, after the reduction of the Royal Navy following Napoleon's defeat, Hayden was lucky to hold on to his position. He journeyed to South America on HMS *Andromache*, defending British interests in the area during the wars of independence of countries such as Argentina, Bolivia, Columbia, Panama, Ecuador and Peru against Spain.

Hayden then joined HMS *Conway* in February 1821 as assisting navigating officer under Captain Basil Hall. After some time, he left the navy, and upon purchasing a brigantine called the *Colonel Allen*, began a career as a trader. When the vice-admiral of Chile, Admiral Lord Thomas Cochrane, was looking for a ship to take him to Brazil, he chose Hayden's brigantine. This would prove fortunate, as Cochrane was to play a significant role in Hayden's life.

In 1821, Brazil's war of independence against Portugal was at its height and its navy was in desperate need of ships. Hayden offered his services and sold his ship to the Brazilians, who rerigged it as a man-o'-war and renamed it *Bahia*, after a military base. Cochrane became Commander-in-Chief of the Brazilian Navy, and Hayden found himself appointed Commander, at Cochrane's side.

Cochrane led a successful campaign against Portugal, and after Hayden captured the Argentine corvette *Libertad del Sur*, he was promoted to Captain of Frigate. He took part in the battles of Quilmes (29–30 July 1826) and Monte Santiago (7–8 April 1827), which witnessed fierce engagements but which proved significant victories for Brazil. (These battles were part of the Cisplatine War, fought between Argentina and Brazil. The Argentine forces were led by fellow Irishman Admiral William Brown.) After the war, Hayden was promoted to Commander of the Brazilian Naval Division of the East.

After Brazil achieved independence from Portugal, the country experienced a series of internal rebellions. Hayden, as commander of the frigates *Imperatriz* and *Campista*, was important in the suppression of the Cabanos rebellion (1835–36). As a result, he was promoted again, this time to the rank of full captain in October 1836. Married since 1829 to Anna de Fonseca Costa, he eventually retired from the navy in 1842.

The young monarch of Brazil, Emperor Pedro II, wanted a modern navy for the newly independent state and, in 1849, Hayden was persuaded to return to the navy, now as Commodore. In 1851, he became a member of the Naval Armaments Commission. Now in his sixties, his adventurous life began to take its toll, and his health was affected. He left Brazil in 1856 for Europe and died in Portsmouth on 17 September 1857.

Thomas Charles Wright.

THOMAS CHARLES WRIGHT

1799–1868

Thomas Charles Wright was an officer in Simón Bolívar's army and the founding father of the Ecuadorian Navy, rising to the rank of Admiral. A hero in Ecuador, he helped to free the country from Spanish rule.

✳

Thomas Wright was born in Queensborough, Drogheda, County Louth, on 26 January 1799. His parents were Joseph Wright and Mary Montgomery. Like many another Irishman, he went into naval training at a young age, and at the tender age of eleven he attended Portsmouth Royal Naval College.

His cadetship began aboard HMS *Newcastle*, under the command of George Stuart. He was fourteen when he sailed to the east coast of America in the squadron of Admiral John Borlase Warren and was engaged in the blockading of ports. When he returned to England in 1817, Wright had attained the rank of midshipman.

Between 1813 and 1817, after the Napoleonic Wars, the Royal Navy dispensed with the services of some 120,000 men. Commissions were few and far between, in particular for a young junior officer of Irish descent. Wright and other like-minded colleagues decided to sail for South America and enlist in Simón Bolívar's revolutionary army, to support local uprisings against Spanish rule. Known as *El Libertador* or the Liberator of America, Bolívar was a great Venezuelan political and military leader and led Colombia, Venezuela, Ecuador, Peru, Panama and Bolivia to independence from the Spanish Empire.

Wright enlisted in the British Legion to fight for Simón Bolívar. He departed Fowey harbour, Cornwall, on 2 January 1818, aboard the *Dowson*, under the command of a Captain Dormer. Wright and 200 fellow volunteers landed in Saint Thomas Island, one of the Virgin Islands, some weeks later.

These volunteers became the Rifles Corps and were sent with Colonel Pigott's 54th Foot and Admiral Luis Brion's squadron to Margarita Island, off the Venezuelan coast, arriving on 21 April 1818.

Bolívar's campaign of liberation began in Apure in Venezuela. Wright, who was inspired by the radical and republican ideas of the time, met *El Libertador* at Angostura and was enormously impressed by him. Wright fought alongside Bolívar as an officer and took part in a legendary trek in New Granada, 1,500 miles over the Andes. In what must have been an unbelievably arduous and treacherous march, a quarter of the British Legion troops perished.

Wright played a significant part in numerous battles, including at Pantano de Vargas and the Battles of Boyacá, Carabobo, Bomboná and Pasto. He played a leading role in the Battle of Boyacá, for which he was promoted to Captain. After the Battle of Bomboná, he was mentioned twice in Bolívar's order of the day, which noted his exceptional courage and skill. In 1823, he was promoted to the rank of Lieutenant Colonel.

Whilst Bolívar cut a giant swathe through the continent, successfully freeing countries, it was clear that he was weak against the might of the Spanish Navy. To improve the situation, General Bolívar appointed Wright to the newly formed United Pacific Naval Squadron. In 1823, the first Ecuadorian naval force was formed, with British naval officer John Illingworth Hunt at the helm. They had three warships: the schooner *Guayaquileña*, the brig *Chimborazo* and the corvette *Pichincha*.

Captain Wright, as he was newly promoted, was given charge of the *Chimborazo* and helped with patrols along the Peruvian coast and in the transportation of troops. He participated in successful campaigns against the Spanish and in the blockade of Callao, a Spanish stronghold.

Proving himself capable, Wright was promoted by Bolívar to Commodore of the Pacific Southern Squadron, with a fleet of ships under his command. In 1824, when Callao capitulated, Spanish rule in South America was effectively at an end. Wright chose to settle in Ecuador, then part of Bolívar's Republic of Gran Colombia.

Wright and Bolívar became close friends in this period, with Wright ferrying the general from port to port. Bolivar was a target and at risk of capture at sea, but he trusted Wright to provide him with safe passage.

Having gained their independence from Spain, the new countries fought amongst themselves over territory, and Peru engaged in battle with Gran Colombia. During the Battle of Punta Malpelo on 31 August 1828, Wright sustained an injury when in command of the *Guayaquileña*, but survived.

Ecuador declared itself a republic in 1830, although both Peru and Gran Colombia claimed parts of it as their territory. After a brief spell in the army, Wright returned to the navy, promoted to the rank of General of Brigade.

Further unsettling the climate, two presidents – Rocafuerte and Valdivieso – both declared they were in charge of Ecuador. A battle took place in Minarica in January 1835, during which Valdivieso's general was defeated. Rocafuerte was sworn in as president and brought some stability to the state.

In 1835, Wright became Commander-in-Chief of the Ecuadorian Navy and is considered its founding father. With political unrest still rife, he spent fifteen years in exile, in Chile and Peru, after the government he supported was overthrown in a coup. However, he returned from exile in 1860.

He married Angelo Rico y Rocafuerte, a niece of the president, and they had five children. She died in 1839, and he married her sister, Maria Josefa Rico y Rocafuerte, in 1844. He died at home on 10 December 1868.

The naval college in Ecuador is named in Wright's honour. Two portraits of him are on display in the Navy Museum in Guayaquil, Ecuador. There are statues to him in Ecuador and a large marble memorial to him in his native Drogheda. Since 2019 there has been a Thomas Charles Wright scholarship programme in the Ecuadorian Naval College, under which the winning two students get to spend eight weeks in Drogheda to learn English. In 1972 and 1999, the Ecuadorian government released stamps in his honour.

Like other Irishmen, Wright found advantage in political upheaval in South America and firmly planted his name amongst the revolutionaries that changed the continent.

Robert Halpin and his dog aboard the *Great Eastern*, designed by
Isambard Kingdom Brunel.

ROBERT HALPIN

1836–1894

Robert Halpin is best known for being the captain of the SS *Great Eastern*, a ship designed by Isambard Kingdom Brunel, which laid transatlantic cable.

*

Halpin was born at the Bridge Tavern in Wicklow on 16 February 1836, the youngest of thirteen children. Born into a family of some prosperity, he went to sea at a young age.

Wicklow town at that time was a very busy port and must have seemed a wonderland to a small child. From all around the world came brigantines, schooners and their crews, who no doubt brought their stories to the local dockside taverns.

Unlike many others, Halpin didn't run away to sea purely out of economic necessity, but signed up for a full apprenticeship. This was countersigned by his father, as Halpin was a minor. Aged eleven, he joined the *Briton*, which left Wicklow for the Canadian territories via London, sailing up the St Laurence River to Quebec and Ottawa. The *Briton*, a brigantine (a small, very fast, two-masted ship with large, square sails), made two voyages a year across the North Atlantic, so by the time he was thirteen years old, Halpin had crossed the ocean four times. On one of these voyages, in 1851, on the return trip from Quebec to Liverpool, the ship was hit with bad weather near Padstow, Cornwall, and was wrecked. All the crew survived; nevertheless, fifteen was a tender age to face what must have been a harrowing experience, and it was an enormous test of character, which no doubt stood to him later.

Halpin transferred to the *Henry Tanner*, which plied the route to Melbourne, Australia. At the time (1852–53), the height of the Australian gold rush, many sailors jumped ship to go digging for gold. This left ships port-bound, with insufficient crew to work them. Halpin, however, did not go that route, and continued to serve his apprenticeship. He made his way serving other vessels: *Boomerang* as third mate and second mate on *Salem*, before transferring to the steamship *Khersonese*.

In 1854, Halpin finished his seven-year apprenticeship and got his first command, on the SS *Propellor*, also a steamship, the days of sail now ending. It was to be a fortunate move. In 1858, he was given command of the *Argo*, a technological wonder of the age. The *Argo* brought Irish immigrants from Galway to the new world via St John's, Newfoundland. Halpin brought her on her maiden voyage. On the return journey, as they passed Cape Race on the southeastern tip of Newfoundland, *Argo* foundered in very dense fog. No lives were lost; however, a board of inquiry suspended Halpin's master's ticket for nine months. Even though he had followed the standard procedure of the time, which was to speed up the ship in fog, the notion being that the bulk of the ship would disperse the fog, he was master of the *Argo*, and the responsibility for its well-being rested with him. Both the trauma of the wreck and the stress of the suspension were to have a huge psychological effect on someone whose progression to this point had only been upward. He had been at sea for eleven years.

After regaining his master's ticket, Halpin worked for the Spanish government, bringing two ships – *Isla de Cuba* and *Isla de Puerto Rico* – to South America. During the American Civil War (1861–65), he ran goods to the Confederate states and returned with cotton to Europe. The army of the Union had blockaded some ports and, at one point, Halpin was captured. He was released after the Battle of Mobile Bay in 1864.

Back in London, the steamship *Great Eastern*, then the world's biggest ship, was being outfitted for a new purpose. She was five times larger than any other ship, with six masts, five funnels, 6,500 yards of sail, two huge paddle wheels, a 24-foot propeller and a coal-carrying capacity of 15,000 tonnes. She was not surpassed in size until the RMS *Titanic* was built, between 1909 and 1911, in Belfast.

Isambard Kingdom Brunel, one of the great engineers of the age, had designed the *Great Eastern* to be a luxury liner.

His three great ship projects were the *Great Western* (1838), designed to sail between Bristol and New York; the *Great Britain* (1844), which is currently on display in Bristol; and the *Great Eastern* (1858), which was bound for Australia. However, the *Great Eastern* ended up on North Atlantic routes, to which she was unsuited. In 1864, she was refitted and was the main vessel charged with the great scientific task of the age: to connect Europe and North America by laying a transatlantic telegraph cable from Valentia Island, County Kerry, to Heart's Content, Newfoundland. The cable was some 2,600 miles long and weighed 6,000 tonnes. *Great Eastern* set out in 1865, with Robert Halpin as the first officer.

Laying the cable was a perilous task, and it broke several times. Two support vessels, which sailed astern, would fish for the broken cable with grappling hooks, bring it to the surface and resplice it. Some 1,800 miles from Valentia, they ran out of cable, so the voyage had to be abandoned. However, funds were raised to try again, and on Halpin's exact coordinates, they found the cable, spliced in the new cable and completed the task in 1866. To suddenly have almost instantaneous communication between Europe and America was one of the greatest feats of the nineteenth century. It used to take a message three weeks by steamer, or up to ten weeks by a sail ship, and now communication took a little over an hour.

With Halpin now commander of the largest ship in the

world, the *Great Eastern* continued to lay cable, including the French transatlantic cable from Brest to Saint Pierre and Miquelon, the Bombay–Aden–Suez cable, the Australia–New Zealand–East Indies cable and the Madras–Singapore–Penang and Madeira–Brazil cables.

For his services to telegraphic communication, Halpin was the recipient of many honours. Emperor Pedro II of Brazil made him Knight of the Order of the Rose. He was elected a Fellow of the Royal Geographical Society and received the French Legion of Honour. He was appointed an honorary Commander in the Royal Naval Reserve. He also earned a small fortune.

In later life, Halpin returned to Wicklow, holding positions with Wicklow Harbour Commissioners. He ran unsuccessfully as a Member of Parliament for East Wicklow as a Unionist in 1892. Now a wealthy man, he built and resided at Tinakilly House (now a hotel), just north of Wicklow town. He was married to Jessica Munn from Newfoundland, and they had three daughters.

Halpin died aged fifty-seven at Tinakilly from gangrene, which resulted from a minor cut when trimming his toenails. He is buried at Wicklow Parish Church. In a short space of time, Halpin helped transform world communication by laying in the region of 26,000 miles of cable, linking four continents.

John de Robeck.

JOHN DE ROBECK

1862–1928

Sir John Michael de Robeck commanded the Allied Naval Force in the Dardanelles, Turkey, during the First World War and rose to the rank of Admiral of the Fleet with the Royal Navy.

*

Born into the aristocracy at Gowran Grange, Naas, County Kildare, on 10 June 1862, John de Robeck was the second son of John Henry Edward Fock, 4th Baron de Robeck, and Sophie Charlotte de Robeck of Burton Hall, County Carlow.

De Robeck's naval cadetship began on HMS Britannia on 15 July 1875 at the tender age of thirteen. As he worked his way up through the ranks, he showed great aptitude as a natural seaman and leader. As early as 1885, he was promoted to Lieutenant and served on the battleship HMS Audacious, the flagship of the Commander-in-Chief, China, in 1886. He then returned to HMS Britannia in a training capacity.

In 1899, Sir Clements Markham had de Robeck on his list of preferred leaders for his Antarctic Expedition of 1902 to 1904, an expedition that would be led by Captain Robert F. Scott.

In 1902, de Robeck was promoted to Captain and was given command of HMS *Warrior*. Other commissions included command of HMS *Carnarvon* and commander of the battleship HMS *Dominion*, in the Channel Fleet. At the age of forty-nine, in 1911, he was promoted to Rear Admiral. He then became Admiral of Patrols and commanded four flotillas of destroyers. He showed great leadership and tenacity in bringing these ships, which would play an important role in the First World War, to a good operating standard.

When war broke out in 1914, de Robeck had command of the 9th cruiser squadron. In 1915, the War Office sent a naval expedition to the Dardanelles Strait with de Robeck as second in command to Sir Sackville Carden of the Eastern Mediterranean Squadron. Vice-Admiral Carden, coincidentally, was also Irish, having been born in Barnane, near Templemore in County Tipperary.

When Carden fell ill, supposedly because his nerve went with the knowledge that his fleet was below par, he was relieved of his command, and responsibility fell to de Robeck to carry out orders, to take the strait by force and capture Constantinople from the Ottoman Turks. He almost succeeded, as the Turks on land ran out of artillery, but when he lost three Allied battleships in the mine-laden straits, he withdrew.

In April 1915, the Royal Navy landed troops at Gallipoli. Ultimately, the campaign proved to be a disaster for the Allied forces of the British Empire, France and the Russian Empire, as the Ottomans were well prepared for an attack. It was especially disastrous for the Anzac forces from Australia and New Zealand. Both the Allies and the Ottomans suffered enormous numbers of casualties, one of the greatest losses of life in the First World War. While it came at a high price, it was a great victory for the Ottomans and subsequently led to the Turkish War of Independence and the declaration in 1923 of the Republic of Turkey, with Mustafa Kemal Atatürk – a commander at Gallipoli – as founder.

John de Robeck organised the evacuation of ground troops from the Gallipoli peninsula in January 1916. With his reputation intact, he was awarded the rank of Knight Commander of the Order of the Bath for his service during the campaign.

He gained further promotion as commander of the 2nd and 3rd Battle Squadrons of the Grand Fleet and in May 1917 was promoted to Vice Admiral. He served in the Mediterranean as Commander-in-Chief and oversaw peace treaty negotiations with Turkey whilst serving as High Commissioner in Constantinople. For his services in the war, he was created a baronet in December 1919. Promotion to Admiral came in March 1920, and he became Commander-in-Chief of the Atlantic Fleet in August 1922. His final promotion, to Admiral of the Fleet, came in November 1925. He married Hilda, Lady Lockhart, in 1922.

De Robeck had numerous honours and awards conferred upon him for his various deeds of heroism and bravery. He died of a heart attack at his home in London on 20 January 1928 and was buried with full military honours at Bembridge cemetery on the Isle of Wight.

The *Daily Sketch* from 7 July 1916, which shows the commanders of the Dardanelles campaign. Vice Admiral de Robeck is third from the left at the top.

Full Story Of The Dardanelles Told For The First Time.

DAILY SKETCH.

GUARANTEED DAILY NETT SALE MORE THAN 1,000,000 COPIES.

No. 1,974.   LONDON, WEDNESDAY, JULY 7, 1915.   [Registered as a Newspaper.]   ONE HALFPENNY.

THE MEN WHO LED THE LANDING IN THE DARDANELLES.

Vice-Admiral de Robeck, whom Sir Ian Hamilton thanked on behalf of the Army.

General Sir Ian Hamilton, who planned and directed the landing of the troops.

General d'Amade turned the landing at Kum Kale from a feint to a great success.

Major-General Braithwaite. "He is the best Chief of Staff I ever had," said Sir Ian.

Captain Walford, R.A. (dead), who won the V.C. at the storming of Seddul-Bahr.

The transport River Clyde, with her sides cut open to provide quick exits for the troops, run in and grounded on the beach.

"**Operations which were crowned with remarkable success.**" In these words, Sir Ian Hamilton, General Commanding the Mediterranean Expeditionary Force, describes the great landing of the Allied forces on the shores of the Dardanelles. His despatch (published on another page) gives for the first time the full story of this great feat of arms. It is a story told in simple language, but every line is a tribute to the gallantry and sacrifice of our soldiers and sailors.—(Lafayette, Barnet, Elliott and Fry, and Abrahams.)

67

ANDREW
CUNNINGHAM
1883–1963

Andrew Cunningham was a combat commander in the Second World War and served as Admiral of the Fleet for the Royal Navy between the years 1943 and 1946.

*

Cunningham was born on 7 January 1883 at 42 Grosvenor Square, Rathmines, Dublin, to Daniel John Cunningham, a professor of Anatomy at Trinity College Dublin, and Elizabeth Cumming Browne. After initial schooling in Dublin, Cunningham attended Edinburgh Academy and then the Naval Academy Preparatory School, Stubbington House, Berkshire. Whilst there, he showed an aptitude for mathematics and seamanship.

He started his naval cadetship aboard HMS *Britannia* in 1897. He saw action during the Second Boer War at Pretoria and Diamond Hill in June 1900, serving in the naval brigade and made his way steadily through the ranks to command the destroyer HMS *Scorpion* during the First World War. He served mainly in the Mediterranean, protecting convoys.

He had a reputation for excellent seamanship. He was highly decorated for his efforts during the war, receiving the Distinguished Service Order and two bars, a military decoration given for gallantry during active combat, the bars representing multiple achievements.

Between the First and Second World Wars, he saw action in the Baltic Sea, in particular in command of the destroyer *Seafire*. German naval forces were trying to undermine the independence of Latvia, which Britain recognised and supported. Rear Admiral Sir Walter Cowan, impressed with Cunningham's navigation in mine-laden seas and his general seamanship, took him on as field officer and chief of staff while serving on the North Americas and West Indies Squadron, based in Bermuda.

In the 1920s, Cunningham returned to Britain to naval college and, after a year there, took command of the battleship *Rodney*. Over 216 metres (710 feet) in length, she had a maximum speed of twenty-three knots. In the early 1930s, Cunningham achieved further promotion and also served as aide de camp to King George V. In 1934, he was appointed Rear Admiral in the Mediterranean and made a Companion of the Bath. Between his forays in the Mediterranean and the North Atlantic, he learnt and showed great skill in night manoeuvres at sea, something that would serve him well in the Second World War.

In 1938, Cunningham was appointed to the Admiralty as Deputy Chief of the Naval Staff. The First Sea Lord, Admiral Sir John Backhouse, succumbed to illness for six months that same year and Cunningham deputised for him on the Committee of Imperial Defence and on the Admiralty Board. This was a crucial time, as Britain was on the verge of war with Germany.

Given his knowledge of the Mediterranean, Cunningham was promoted to Commander-in-Chief of the Mediterranean Fleet in June 1939, some three months before Britain officially entered the war. He knew that protecting the small British naval base on Malta, and the convoys that supplied it, was everything. There is an old expression, 'He who controls Malta, controls the Mediterranean.' The country was in a precarious position, surrounded by Axis-controlled territory, and Cunningham feared the Italian Navy in particular, as they had a large fleet and a great knowledge of the Mediterranean, and Italian-controlled Sicily was just over fifty nautical miles from Malta. Malta was one of the most intensively bombed areas during the whole war. The Luftwaffe and Regia Aeronautica of Italy dropped over 6,500 bombs on the grand harbour area alone.

During the war, Cunningham negotiated the decommissioning of Force X, the French naval squadron at Alexandria, after the fall of France to the Axis powers. He made sure that all the crews were repatriated.

However, the threat of an Italian naval attack was still to

the forefront of his mind, not only on Malta, but also on British interests in North Africa. Taranto, a naval base in the heel of Italy, housed a large proportion of the Italian fleet: six battleships, seven heavy cruisers, two light cruisers and eight destroyers. The navy, with the aircraft carrier HMS *Illustrious*, carried out a surprise attack on Taranto that began on 11 November 1940. The first all-aircraft naval attack in history, with planes flying from HMS *Illustrious*, it was a huge success. Another attack against the Italians at the Battle of Cape Matapan in March 1941, where Cunningham's forces put three Italian cruisers out of action, firmly established British dominance over the Italian Navy.

During the bombardment of Crete in May 1941 by the Luftwaffe, Cunningham's fleet rescued 16,500 of 22,000 Allied forces, albeit at the loss of three cruisers and six destroyers.

In 1942/43, Cunningham served under US General Dwight D. Eisenhower, who esteemed him highly. Eisenhower made him naval commander of the Allied Expeditionary Force. In this capacity, Cunningham commanded the large fleet that covered the Allied invasion of French North Africa in November 1942 (Operation Torch). In January 1943, he was promoted to Admiral of the Fleet, a five-star naval officer rank and the highest rank of the Royal Navy. He was present in Malta on 11 September 1943 to see the Italian fleet surrender. In October 1943, he was assigned to a desk job, becoming First Sea Lord and chief of the Naval Staff, with responsibility for the strategic direction of the navy for the rest of the war. He reported directly to Prime Minister Winston Churchill, and attended all the major conferences of the war going forward, including Potsdam and Yalta. At Yalta, Germany and Berlin were divided into four Allied zones, which later became East and West Germany, and an Irishman was in the middle of it all!

Cunningham was made a member of the peerage as Baron Cunningham of Hyndhope, and at the end of the war he helped the Royal Navy transition to peace. He retired as First Sea Lord in May 1945, and later that year was made Viscount Cunningham of Hyndhope. In retirement, he held several appointments and acted as Lord High Steward at the coronation of Queen Elizabeth II in 1953. He published his autobiography, *A Sailor's Odyssey*, in 1951. He died in London on 12 June 1963 and was buried at sea off Plymouth.

The Yalta conference, where the future of postwar Europe was decided. Seated (l–r): Winston Churchill, Franklin D. Roosevelt and Joseph Stalin. Andrew Cunningham stands behind and to the left of Churchill.

James Vincent Forrestal (seated) and Chester W. Nimitz of US Naval High Command.

JAMES FORRESTAL

1892–1949

James Forrestal, whose father came from Mayo, was the last cabinet-level United States Secretary of the Navy and the first United States Secretary of Defense.

✻

James Vincent Forrestal was born in Matteawan, New York, the son of James Forrestal, who left a small cottage at the foot of Nephin, County Mayo, to emigrate to America where he found success, running a construction firm.

The Forrestals home-schooled their three sons, raising them in a very strict Catholic environment. Their youngest, James, rejected the disciplinary nature of this. Working initially as a local reporter, he put himself through Princeton University and joined the naval reserves. He served as a staff officer and left active duty with the navy at the end of the First World War.

Forrestal changed direction and sold bonds on Wall Street, where he made his fortune. He survived the crash of 1929 and came to the attention of government by giving testimony at Capitol Hill about stock market reform. In his spare time, he worked as a publicist for the Democratic Party in New York, helping local politicians to win elections, including one Franklin D. Roosevelt, who was a neighbour.

Forrestal showed great skill as an administrator. In 1940, Roosevelt appointed him Under Secretary of the Navy. The world was at war, and Forrestal proved to be hugely efficient in industrialising America for this effort, and reforming Pearl Harbor. When Frank Knox, the Secretary of the Navy, died of a heart attack in April 1944, Forrestal stepped into his shoes and led America through the closing years of the war. He led a policy of racial integration in the US Navy, another defining moment of modernisation.

Nor did Forrestal shy away from action: he spent time on battlefields, and witnessed the infamous Battle of Iwo Jima. He was deeply moved when US marines raised the Stars and Stripes atop Mount Suribachi – the first time the American flag was raised on Japanese soil – a moment immortalised by Joe Rosenthal's iconic photograph.

Forrestal eventually helped to negotiate peace terms for Japan's unconditional surrender, along with War Secretary Henry Stimson, Chief of Staff William Leahy, and Assistant Secretary of War John McCloy, pushing for a softer policy that would allow a negotiated armistice. Concerned with the threat of Soviet Communism in the chaotic aftermath of the war, he was a huge influence on and supporter of Senator Joseph McCarthy.

Forrestal knew Joseph Kennedy, and in 1945 he accompanied his son John F. Kennedy to a war-torn Germany. JFK's descendants hailed from New Ross, County Wexford. Forrestal's ancestors came from near the same area before they were sent to Connacht after the 1641 Rebellion. The two men had plenty in common, not least that their respective roles were important in the history of America.

In 1946, Forrestal witnessed the detonation of the atomic bomb at a test in the Marshall Islands. Stunned by its power, he participated in the development of the National Security Act of 1947, which changed and strengthened US foreign policy.

In 1947, he was appointed the first US Secretary of Defense, under President Harry S. Truman. A workaholic all his life, Forrestal continued to push for racial integration in the military services, and a government policy was eventually implemented in 1949.

Things soured towards him somewhat when he was vocally opposed to the creation of the state of Israel. Prophetically, he believed that a partition of Palestine would prove enormously problematic. His stance incensed many around him and damaged his relationship with Truman. These tensions and the toll of the pressure of his position culminated in his resignation in 1949.

Exhausted and broken from work, he entered psychiatric treatment in the National Naval Medical Centre in Bethesda, Maryland. He was diagnosed with severe depression and his treatment included insulin shock therapy (he narrowly avoided electroconvulsive therapy). His recovery was slow but progressive. However, two months after his admittance, he fell or jumped from a window in his room on the sixteenth floor to his death. There have been several theories that suggest he was 'helped' in his death, including assassination by the CIA for his stance on Israel, or that he was murdered by communists. The report of his death omitted the fact that a cord had initially been tied around his neck, information not released by Department of the Navy records until 2004.

Forrestal's diaries from 1944 to 1949 were published in 1951 and serialised in the *New York Herald Tribune*, although they were heavily censored. The originals were published in 2001.

President Truman awarded him the Distinguished Service Medal and Medal of Merit in his lifetime. His legacy left his name to the James V. Forrestal Building in Washington, D.C., and the aircraft carrier USS *Forrestal*, which operated during the Vietnam War and in Operation Desert Storm.

He had married Josephine Ogden, at one stage a writer for *Vogue* magazine, and the couple had two children, Michael and Peter. Michael served in the Kennedy Administration. Peter worked in banking and settled back in Ireland.

Forrestal's epitaph on his tomb in Arlington Cemetery reads 'In the great cause of good government' and epitomises a man who rose from humble origins to lead one of the great offices of state, at a time when America, and the world, needed it most.

A complex individual with strident opinions, James Forrestal was nonetheless one of the characters instrumental in Allied victory in the Second World War.

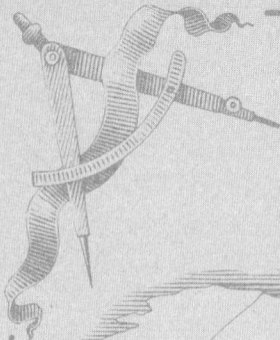

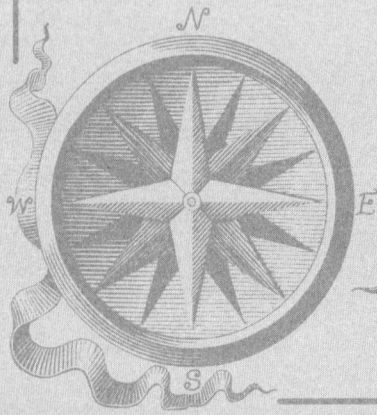

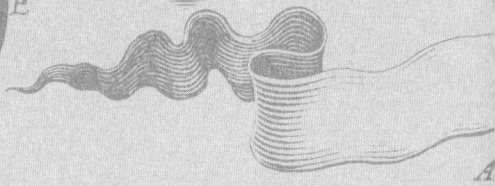

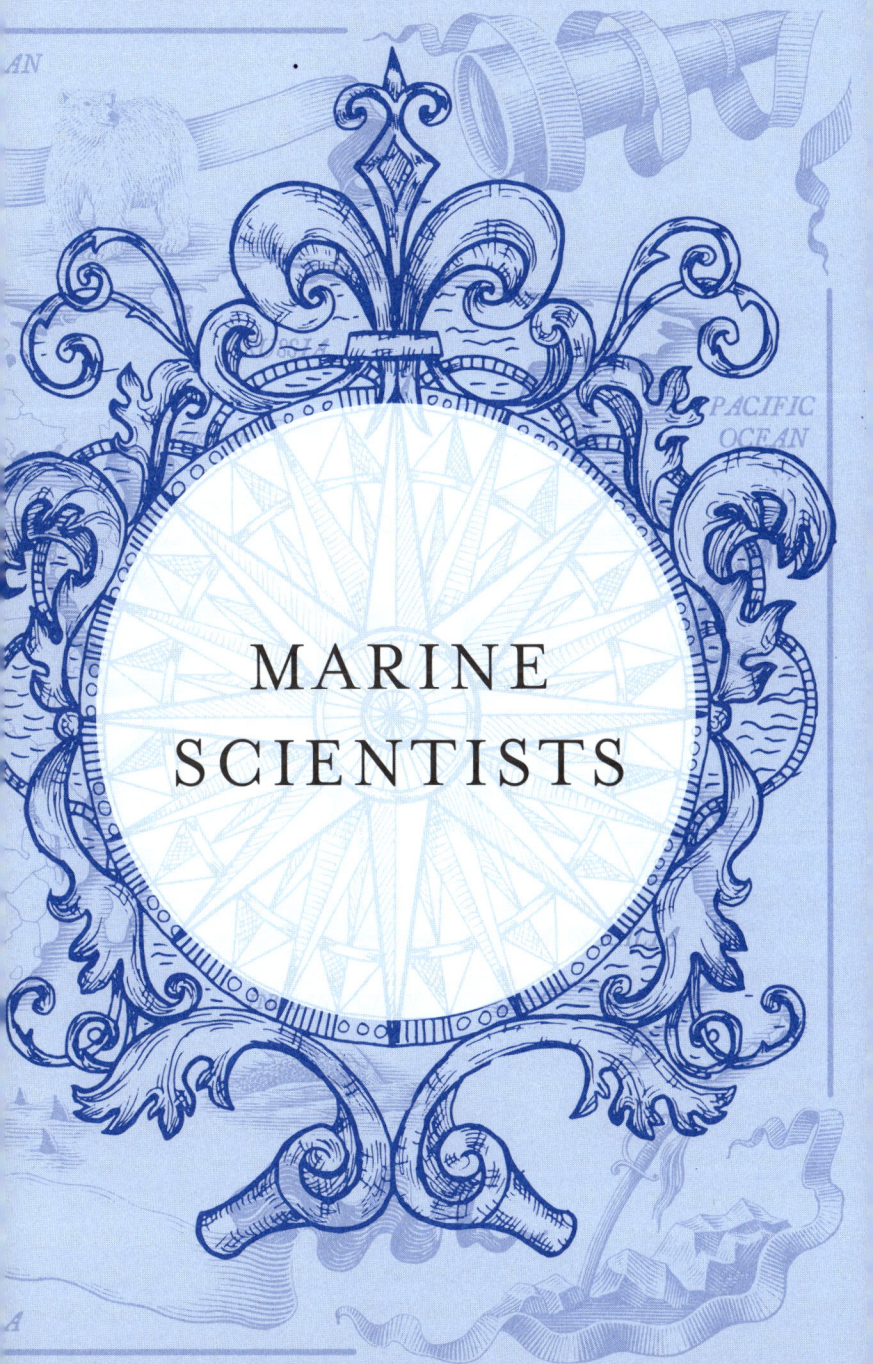

MARINE SCIENTISTS

FRANCIS BEAUFORT

1774–1857

Born in Flower Hill, Navan, County Meath, on 27 May 1774, the son of a Navan rector, Francis Beaufort found fame as a hydrographer and as inventor of the Beaufort wind scale. A noted naval officer, his career culminated in the rank of Rear Admiral.

✱

Beaufort's family were descended from Huguenots who had fled religious persecution in France in the sixteenth century. The whole family had an interest in the pursuit of science: his father, Daniel, produced the first maps of Ireland using the scale of six inches to one mile and was a founding member of the Royal Irish Academy; Francis' sister Harriet was a botanist and wrote about the subject for children.

After attending David Bates Military and Naval Academy in Dublin, Beaufort studied at Trinity College Dublin under Dr Henry Ussher, a professor of Astronomy. He spent time at the Dunsink Observatory, Castleknock, and would have studied the earth, the moon and its effect on the tides.

At the age of fourteen, he went on a surveying expedition to

Indonesia on the British East India Company's East Indiaman *Vansittart*. The ship was wrecked; however, only one life was lost. The wreck was blamed on poor sea charts for the area, something which had a huge influence on the young man. It became his life's work: to value, and have others value, the importance of accurate charts for those risking their lives at sea.

Beaufort began his career with the Royal Navy in 1790, and gradually made his way up the ranks. He served on HMS *Aquilon* during the French Revolutionary War in 1794, and was promoted to lieutenant in 1796 on HMS *Phaeton*. He was badly injured in an operation off Malaga and promoted to Commander. During his recuperation, he worked on a semaphore line, or optical telegraph, between Dublin and Galway with his brother-in-law, Richard Lovell Edgeworth. This was a system of communication based on visual signals between a line of towers. Beaufort spent two years on the project, without payment. It showed his dedication to science.

As he continued his ascent through the ranks, Beaufort used his free time to study astronomy, to take bearings and depth soundings of water and to measure shorelines, the results of which he drew onto charts. Eventually, at the age of fifty-five, he was appointed Chief Hydrographer to the Admiralty. He stayed in the post for twenty-six years, during which time he collaborated with several navies throughout the world to produce charts of the planet's oceans.

Drawn by F. Beaufort.   SELINTY *formerly* TRAJANOPOLIS.   Engraved by G. Cooke.

An 1817 engraving by G. Cooke, based on a drawing by Francis Beaufort.

Beaufort and his teams' charts revolutionised marine navigation. As a result of his work, there was a greater understanding and visualisation of what lay beneath the waves. Underwater mountains and cliffs were all revealed on charts.

To take depth soundings, a vessel at sea discharged a rope with a lead weight attached. When the lead hit the sea floor, the line was marked. The depth was measured in fathoms (one fathom is six foot). Sometimes tar was attached to the weight, to determine the type of bottom, whether it was sandy, stony, rocky or shale-like. It was only in the early 1920s that this method was superseded by echo sounding, which uses soundwaves, measurements being taken by how long it takes for the sound to echo off the bottom, determining depth.

Beaufort, in his position as Chief Hydrographer, helped to further the importance of science in naval and marine life. His tenure coincided with an age of scientific discovery.

He trained Robert Fitzroy, who was in charge of the second voyage of HMS *Beagle*, famous for having Charles Darwin as a man of science on board. Darwin drew on his discoveries to formulate his theory of evolution, as presented in his book *On the Origin of Species*. Beaufort helped James Clark Ross to get funding for an expedition to the Antarctic, where Ross measured the Earth's magnetic field. Beaufort was also responsible for publishing the first edition of the *Admiralty Tide Tables* in 1833.

Beaufort is best known, however, for creating a method to describe wind strength based on the appearance of the sea. The Beaufort wind scale is still used today. Knowing how strong the wind is, and indeed how strong it will become, is of absolute importance to the mariner.

Initially, the cipher related to how the wind affected the sails of a frigate, and it had thirteen divisions, but as shipping moved on to steam, it changed to how the sea, rather than the sails, behaved in wind, and it now has twelve divisions.

In the 1940s, the Beaufort scale was extended and forces 13 to 17 were added. They apply to special cases, such as tropical cyclones, and are generally used only in Taiwan and China. The scale is used throughout the world.

Beaufort retired from the Royal Navy in 1846, aged seventy-two. He had a huge amount of correspondence and diaries during his life, a lot of it written in code. He was married initially to Alicia Magdalena Wilson, and after she died in 1834, he married Honora Edgeworth in 1838. He died on 17 December 1857 in Hove, Sussex, aged eighty-three. The Beaufort Sea in the Arctic and Beaufort Island in the Antarctic are named in his honour.

BEAUFORT WIND SCALE		
BEAUFORT NUMBER	WIND SPEED (MPH)	SAILOR'S TERM
0	Under 1	Calm
1	1–3	Light air
2	4–7	Light breeze
3	8–12	Gentle breeze
4	13–18	Moderate breeze
5	19–24	Fresh breeze
6	25–31	Strong breeze
7	32–38	Moderate gale
8	39–46	Fresh gale
9	47–54	Strong gale
10	55–63	Whole gale
11	64–72	Storm
12	73 or higher	Hurricane force

JOHN PHILIP
HOLLAND

1841–1914

Engineer John Philip Holland is considered the father of the modern submarine. His invention was the first underwater vessel accepted by the US Navy.

*

Holland was born in Liscannor, County Clare, on 24 February 1841. His father, John Senior, was a member of the Royal Coastguard Service. His mother, Máire Ní Scannlán, was a native Irish speaker, and he grew up speaking Irish, learning English only when he went to school. He lived with his parents and three brothers in a coastguard cottage in Liscannor.

When he finished his schooling, he joined the Irish Christian Brothers in Limerick and worked as a teacher in various places, including Limerick, Cork, Drogheda and Enniscorthy. He taught mathematics in Coláiste Rís in Dundalk, County Louth.

Holland never took his final vows, and left the Christian Brothers because of ill health. He emigrated to America in

1873 to live with his brother Michael, who was a member of the American Fenian Brotherhood. He worked initially in engineering, but returned to teaching for six years in St John's Catholic School in Paterson, New Jersey.

When not teaching, Holland worked on ideas and designs for a submarine – a naval vessel that can propel itself both beneath the water and on the surface – and submitted some initial designs to the US Navy for consideration, but they were dismissed as unworkable. He got some financial support from the Irish Fenian Society, however, which allowed him to resign his teaching post eventually. The Fenians hoped to use a submarine against the British.

Holland's first submarine, the *Fenian Ram*, was launched in 1881. It was the world's first practical submarine. It had a Brayton Ready Motor that used kerosene. It was able both to dive and submerge successfully, and was armed with a gun, 3.3 metres (11 feet) in length, which fired from the bow.

Defective riveting meant that it could not stay down for a sustained period. An extraordinary feat of engineering, it nevertheless ended Holland's relationship with the Fenians, as there was an issue with payment to him. The *Fenian Ram* is preserved in the Paterson Museum, New Jersey.

Holland continued to work on his designs, especially on the matter of getting the submersible to cover distance: it wasn't enough just to sink and come to the surface again. In

1895, his newly formed J.P. Holland Torpedo Boat Company eventually won a contract from the US Navy to build a submarine. The *Holland VI*, as it was called initially, was launched on 17 May 1897. For the first time, a submarine had power to run submerged for a considerable distance. It combined the use of an electric motor when submerged and a petrol engine when on the surface. It impressed the US Navy enough that they bought it, tested it rigorously and, on 12 October 1900, commissioned it as USS *Holland*.

The vessel was sixteen metres long, displaced seventy-four tonnes and had a gun that could fire a 45kg projectile over half a kilometre. The hull was cigar-shaped and, as with submarine design going forward, the tanks were flooded for submersion. It had a device that could take it to a predetermined depth and another balancing element that kept it level. The petrol engine that powered it on the surface also ran a generator that charged the batteries for the electric motor used when it was below the surface. Its surface speed was seven knots.

The US Navy commissioned seven more, which were built in New Jersey and California. The company that produced them eventually became General Dynamics, a defence and aerospace company (currently the fifth-largest defence contractor in the world). The design was revolutionary and adopted by other naval powers. The Royal Navy developed the Holland class submarine. The Royal Navy's HMS *Holland 1* is on display at the Submarine Museum in Gosport, Hampshire, England. The Imperial Japanese Navy based their first five submarines on Holland's design, but made theirs longer. Holland went on to design the *Holland II* and *Holland III* prototypes. He also designed the *Holland IV* or the *Zalinski*, financed by US Army Lieutenant Edmund Zalinski.

Holland was a man of great ingenuity: he also developed a motor truck and was an amateur astronomer and musician. It has also been suggested that he toyed with designs for flying machines.

In 1887, Holland married Margaret Foley, and they had five children. He died on 12 August 1914, in the early months of the First World War. He is buried in Totowa, New Jersey, near where he launched his first submarine.

Holland's invention changed naval warfare. Submarines were used initially during the First World War, with Germany, in particular, using them to great effect and devastation. The primary weapon of the submarine is the torpedo, a self-propelled missile. Submarines are used also to rescue pilots downed over water. In the Second World War, American submarines were instrumental in helping to destroy the Imperial Japanese Navy fleet.

There is a statue to Holland in Drogheda, on the site of the school where he taught and first had his dreams of building a submarine.

MAUDE DELAP

1866–1953

ANNIE MASSEY

1868–1931

Aself-taught marine biologist, Maude Delap was the first person to observe and describe the full life cycle of jellyfish. She also undertook an extensive study of plankton from the coast around Valentia Island, County Kerry, thus enriching our knowledge of life in the seas. Her work on plankton is still referred to today for the insight it gives on plankton communities, of which there are many in Irish waters.

*

Delap was born in Templecrone Rectory, County Donegal. Her father was the Reverend Alexander Delap and her mother was Anna Jane Goslett. Her family, including her nine siblings, moved to Valentia Island in Kerry, when her father took up the post of rector to the island and Cahirciveen in 1874. Her brothers were encouraged in formal education, but she and her sisters were not. Both Maude and her sister Constance were interested in nature; their father, an amateur naturalist, encouraged them in this.

Valentia, with its windswept wildness, is a haven for wildlife and it fascinated Delap. Both she and Constance collected prolific numbers of specimens from the area, which are now housed in the Natural History Museum in Dublin. They would often row out in a boat and use a tow line to collect specimens.

As a result of their endeavours, a survey was undertaken by the Royal Irish Academy. Edward T. Browne of University College London took charge of the survey in 1895 and 1896. Encouraged by this, the Delap girls continued collecting specimens and started to record sea temperatures and changes in marine life in the area. They were inspired by their surroundings and endeavoured to study it in great detail. Delap corresponded with Browne for years and sent him many drawings of her findings.

Jellyfish in particular fascinated her, and she bred them in a makeshift laboratory at home in hand-made aquariums, where she observed their life cycles. Her work on the compass jellyfish and the blue jellyfish was published. It was her pioneering work and identified for the first time the different life stages of both species.

It was an extraordinary moment for marine biology

Edwardsia Delapiae, a sea anemone named in Maude Delap's honour.

and, because of it, Delap was offered a fellowship in the Plymouth Marine Biological Station in 1906, a great honour. Unfortunately for Delap, her father forbade her attendance. Even though she was forty at this stage, it must have been a devastating blow.

Undeterred, she continued to study the natural world around her. She identified a True's beaked whale when it washed up on the island. This particular species of whale was known only from an incomplete specimen found in America. She collected plankton between 1906 and 1910, and published a paper on it in 1924.

In 1936, Delap was made a fellow of the Linnean Society of London, a society dedicated to the study of natural history. She continued to work on Valentia until her death in 1953.

Edwardsia Delapiae is a sea anemone named in her honour, a species she first recorded on the coast at Valentia. It is rare; outside of Valentia it has been spotted just once in Scotland and once in Norway. A plaque was erected to her in 1998 on Valentia by the Irish National Committee for Commemorative Plaques in Science and Technology.

*

Another woman working in this largely male-dominated field, with whom Maude Delap collaborated at one time, was Annie Letitia Massey. Born in Hampshire on 29 January

1868, she grew up in Malahide near the mollusc-collecting area known as the Velvet Strand. She was another self-taught marine biologist and was recognised internationally for her knowledge of molluscs.

Massey had a huge interest in the natural world and, in 1885, aged eighteen, she observed the first pair of nesting redstarts in Ireland at Powerscourt Estate in Wicklow. She contributed regularly to the *Irish Naturalist* journal. She was a founding member of the Irish Society for the Protection of Birds. Because of her reputation in identifying marine species, she was sent specimens from all over the world, not least by the Terra Nova Antarctic Expedition of 1910–1913, led by Captain Robert Falcon Scott.

There was a common misconception that oysters could be aged via the rings on their shells, but Massey's study of over 600 species proved this was not the case and her findings were published.

Four species of molluscs, specifically cephalopods (animals such as squid or octopus), have been named after her: *Opisthoteuthis massyae*, *Pholidoteuthis massyae*, *Bolitaena massyae* and *Eledone massyae*.

A quiet, retiring person, she died in Howth on 17 April 1931.

Both Maude Delap and Annie Massey have inspired countless marine biologists, and have strengthened our understanding of the oceans.

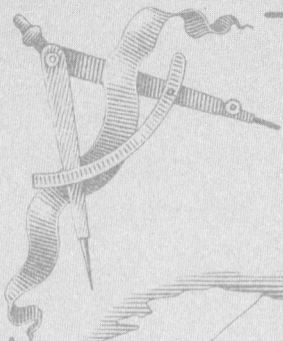

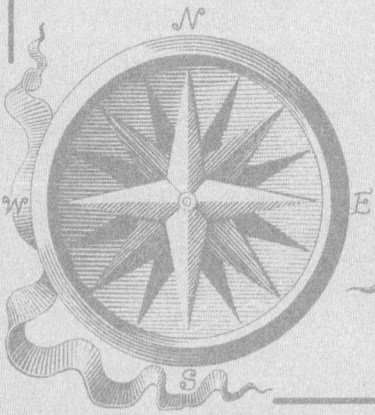

PIRATES

Granuaile at the fabled meeting with Queen Elizabeth I, from *Anthologia Hibernica*, vol. 11, 1793.

GRANUAILE

c. 1530 – c. 1603

Granuaile – Grace O'Malley, the Pirate Queen – was a notorious Irish pirate from the sixteenth century, known for her plundering activities off the west coast of Ireland. Her exploits not only annoyed the neighbouring clans, but brought her to the attention of the English authorities. Nevertheless, she navigated her way through life with determination and skill, to become leader of the O'Malley clan and command the loyalty of hundreds of fighting mariners.

*

Born the daughter of Eóghan Dubhdara Ó Máille (which translates as Black Oak O'Malley), Granuaile took over the leadership of the clan on land and sea when he died. When she was born, around 1530, Henry VIII as the King of England was also the Lord of Ireland. Under English policy, the Irish clans were more or else left alone, but as the Tudors strengthened their grip on the country, this was to change.

The O'Malleys were one of the great seafaring clans of Connacht, based in Clew Bay, County Mayo. They had large fortifications in the form of castles all along the Mayo coast. From these castles, the clan demanded rent from the fishermen who worked the waters, including some from as far away as England. There is a story that Granuaile wanted to go to Spain with her father when she was quite young, but her father was against it, saying her long hair would get caught in the ropes. To defy him, she cut off her hair, and he had no option but to take her. Whether true or not, it tells of a feisty and determined young woman. From this act she is said to have earned her name, from *maol*, meaning bald, but probably more accurately it comes from Gráinne of Umhall, an area in Connacht where the O'Malleys had a stronghold.

In 1546, before she was twenty, Granuaile married Battling Donal O'Flaherty. It was a political alliance between two previously warring clans. (The O'Flahertys had slaughtered many O'Malleys at a supposed peace conference 200 years previously, and the O'Malleys had responded by plundering the O'Flaherty riches.) The O'Flahertys ruled most of wild Connemara and were a constant threat to the merchants of Galway.

The couple had three children: Eóghan, Méadhbh and Murchadh. Donal died in 1565, killed in an ambush by the Joyce clan. Granuaile returned to Mayo and made her main residence on Clare Island. From here, she began pillaging vessels all along the western seaboard. She believed it was a case of pillage or be pillaged, survive or die.

Granuaile's seafaring troops raided the coastline from Valentia Island in the southwest to the far reaches of Ulster in the northwest, and even over towards the Hebrides off the coast of Scotland. Her ships each carried some forty men and the larger ones carried seventy. No one knows how many ships she had, but probably somewhere between three and twenty. They stole mainly cattle, which were a symbol of great wealth.

In 1566, Granuaile married Iron Richard Bourke. The Bourkes were another seafaring family in Mayo. Richard's nickname is said to have come from his ironworks at Burrishoole in Mayo. The pair had a son, called Tibbot or Toby, allegedly born at sea. Richard's castle, Rockfleet, became Granuaile's home and is the castle most associated with her to this day. Her raiding continued, notably against the MacMahon clan.

Around this period, Irish clans had to take part in the 'surrender and regrant' mechanism, where their power structure of clan loyalty would be replaced with a loyalty to England. This was all part of the encroachment of the Tudor dynasty on Ireland. But Mayo was a long way from Dublin, and Granuaile managed to stay out of reach of the Lord Deputy, Sir Henry Sidney. By the late 1570s, she found herself with a price on her head of £500, a considerable sum at the time. She was captured off the coast of Kerry and incarcerated in Dublin Castle for a period, and when released shortly afterwards, resumed her sea raiding. In March 1579, a force from Galway, led by Sheriff William Martin, tried to seize Rockfleet, but was defeated and fled.

Richard Bourke received a knighthood in 1581, and suddenly Granuaile was Lady Bourke. However, this did not stop her raiding, and when Richard died, she partnered up with her son-in-law, Richard 'The Devil's Hook' Bourke. The next few years saw battles between Granuaile and the Crown.

The new President of Connacht, Richard Bingham, was one of the new Puritan military men and he took a particular dislike to Granuaile, a woman who had, in his eyes, overstepped the part of womanhood. A low point came when English troops murdered her son Eóghan and arrested Granuaile. She was brought to the gallows but was reprieved at the last minute.

Bingham continued to make inroads into Granuaile's lands, and a particular blow occurred when her son Murchadh O'Flaherty partnered with him. Granuaile was now in her sixties. She wrote to Henry VIII's daughter, Queen Elizabeth I, asking for a royal pardon and a pension, promising to fight on Elizabeth's behalf in return. Now a true enemy, Bingham had her son Toby thrown in prison, and Granuaile patiently awaited the Queen's response.

The two queens reputedly met in Greenwich Castle in September 1593, although there is little evidence that they met face to face. Both were older women in positions of power, in a man's world, and there is no doubt that each was intrigued by the other. Despite Bingham writing to court and blaming Granuaile for forty years of rebellion in Ireland, Elizabeth looked favourably on Granuaile, granting Toby his freedom and having his mother's lands returned to her.

Bingham had made himself few friends in Connacht. In 1596, he fled to England without permission, fearing for his life, and was imprisoned in the Fleet. He suffered ill-health for the rest of his life and died early in 1599.

The details of Granuaile's death are not known, but it is likely that she died around 1603 in Rockfleet Castle. Elizabeth I also died that year. King James I knighted Granuaile's son Toby, who later became Viscount Mayo under Charles I. There is a story that Granuaile left all her pirate gold to the Cistercian order.

Granuaile's hunger for survival and success in a male-dominated world, during a period of historical turbulence, shows a person of extraordinary strength and resolve. Unlike other lady pirates who came a century later, like Anne Bonny and Mary Read, Granuaile did not feel the need to disguise herself as a man. She was a sea lord, a warrior, a politician, a mother, a daughter, a grandmother and a matriarch. Her name is the stuff of legend, and she is a unique Irish cultural icon.

Anne Bonny. From *A General History of the Pyrates* by Captain Charles Johnson and Daniel Defoe (1724).

ANNE BONNY

c. 1698–1782

Kinsale-born Anne Bonny gained notoriety in the Caribbean as a pirate, one of the few female pirates in history. She is often associated with the infamous pirate Jack Rackham.

*

Bonny was born sometime around 1698, near the Old Head of Kinsale. Most of what we know about her comes from Captain Charles Johnson's book of 1724, *A General History of the Pyrates*, which contains as much fiction as fact. Anne's father was a lawyer from Cork, William Cormac, and her mother, Mary Brennan, was his housemaid. With the scandal of the pregnancy, Anne's father left for America, with Mary and baby Anne in tow.

William did well in America and after some time bought a plantation near Charleston in the colony of Carolina. According to Johnson, Anne was considered both fiery and feisty. There are stories that she stabbed a servant when in a rage, and gave a would-be rapist a severe beating.

Anne married James Bonny, a sailor, in 1718 and took his last name. Anne's father did not approve of the match, as

Bonny was penniless, so the couple moved to the Bahamas, considered a safe haven for pirates. It was here that James reportedly worked for Governor Woodes Rogers as an informant, leading to the arrest of many pirates, something Anne disliked.

The capital of the Bahamas, Nassau on New Providence, was considered more or less lawless, and there were many characters of ill repute there, including Jack Rackham and another woman pirate, Mary Read, who dressed as a man. It was essentially pirate central. 'Calico' Jack, as he was known because of his taste for unusual trousers, made his base on New Providence. When Rackham and Anne met, he already had a reputation, having plundered several vessels at sea. It is said that he designed the infamous skull-and-crossbones pirate flag. They became lovers, and sailed off together in a ship called the *William* that they, along with Mary Read, stole from the quayside through some clever high jinks.

Once at sea, Anne dressed like a man, sporting wide trousers, a shirt and a tunic. They took other crew aboard, but only Rackham and Read knew she was a woman. They spent years around Jamaica. Anne took part in raids as much as the men did and, according to Johnson's account, she was always the last to yield. Anne gave birth to Jack's child in Cuba, but returned to her pirate ways before long.

In September 1720, a proclamation was announced,

declaring that Rackham and his gang were enemies of the Crown, and sea captains as far away as Boston were put on notice of the marauding pirates around New Providence.

Eventually, their reign of terror came to an end as, in November 1720, a Captain Barnet intercepted the crew near Point Negril in southwestern Jamaica. The pirates gave little resistance, some being quite drunk. As the lawmen approached and drew alongside, the only ones left fighting on deck were Anne Bonny, Mary Read and one other pirate; all the others had fled below. The sloop *William* was taken and brought into Port Royal, Jamaica. Rackham was brought ashore in chains.

On 18 November, Rackham and four of the crew were convicted and hanged. Rackham's body was hanged from a gibbet at Plumb Point, a nearby promontory. At his trial, Bonny is said to have declared, 'If he had fought like a man, he need not have been hanged like a dog.' The two women were also put on trial. At the last minute, both declared they were with child. Judge Sir Nicolas Lawes, who was about to pass sentence, halted proceedings and demanded a medical examination. He would allow them to live until they gave birth, albeit in prison.

Mary Read died along with her unborn child in a filthy Jamaican dungeon, having caught a fever. Bonny, however, had an advantage, as many of the Jamaican planters had known her father. However, the fact that she had left her husband counted against her. In the end, unsure what to do with her, the authorities allowed her to leave when her father organised safe passage for her to Carolina.

Bonny gave birth in peace and eventually married a man called Joseph Burleigh, with whom she had eight children. They settled in Charleston. It is believed Bonny died at the ripe old age of eighty-four in April 1782.

POLAR
EXPLORERS

A daguerreotype from 1845 of Francis Rawdon Moira Crozier, an Irish officer of the Royal Navy and explorer who participated in six expeditions to the Arctic and Antarctic.

FRANCIS CROZIER

1796 – c. 1848

Born in Banbridge, County Down, Francis Crozier was a veteran polar explorer who, as captain of HMS *Terror*, was lost at the Northwest Passage, along with all of his crew, as part of the Franklin Expedition.

*

Francis Crozier was the eleventh of thirteen children. His father, George, was a solicitor. A prosperous Presbyterian family, they lived in Avonmore House in the centre of Banbridge and Francis attended school locally. When he was thirteen, he volunteered for the Royal Navy, and slowly made his way up through the ranks.

One of the ships he served on was HMS *Briton*, which visited Pitcairn Island in 1814. There he met the last surviving members of the infamous HMS *Bounty*, the crew of which mutinied against Captain William Bligh. (A little-known fact is that the same William Bligh was responsible for the charting of Dublin Bay.)

As with most young sailors, Crozier had the opportunity to see the world, and in 1821 he got his first taste of the

Arctic, aboard William Parry's HMS *Fury*. It was Parry's second expedition to search for the Northwest Passage.

The Northwest Passage is a sea route connecting the Atlantic and Pacific oceans via the Arctic Ocean. For hundreds of years, since the days of Christopher Columbus in the late 1490s, sailors have struggled to find an alternative route to Asia from Europe, one that avoids Cape Horn and the Cape of Good Hope. An ice-bound route was eventually found and credited to Wexford man Robert McClure in 1850 (see pages 119–23). Regular marine shipping is not possible throughout the year, but as the climate changes and the ice melts, the waters are becoming increasingly navigable.

Parry's expedition failed. He made two more attempts, with Crozier accompanying, both of which also failed, but Crozier at least made the rank of Lieutenant and gained valuable experience in the ice. In 1827, he was elected to the Royal Astronomical Society for his studies on magnetic fields with Parry. He also became great friends with the flamboyant explorer James Clark Ross. Crozier served with Ross on other vessels and made the rank of Commander in 1837.

In 1839, Ross led the Ross Expedition to Antarctica, a four-year exploratory and scientific endeavour. Two ships brought them there, HMS *Erebus* and HMS *Terror*. Crozier was in command of HMS *Terror*. They went the furthest south yet, and made many discoveries, namely the Ross Sea, Ross Island, the Ross Ice Shelf and Mount Erebus. On their return in 1843, Crozier was elected a fellow of the Royal Society, in recognition of his contribution to scientific and polar exploration.

In 1845, Crozier joined the ill-fated Franklin Expedition, once again searching for the fabled Northwest Passage. Captain Sir John Franklin was a veteran of the Napoleonic Wars, and he led the expedition in command of HMS *Erebus*, whilst Crozier captained HMS *Terror*. When Franklin died in June 1847, Crozier had full command, with James Fitzjames taking over the captaincy of *Erebus*.

No one knew what had happened to Franklin and the other expedition members. The last sighting of the ships had been in July 1845, when they were spotted by a whaler. Franklin's wife, Jane, pressured the Admiralty to send a search party. After several attempts, in 1848 a search party, led by Francis McClintock (an Irishman born in Dundalk, County Louth, and a polar explorer in his own right) and aided by local Inuit, discovered a note written by Crozier and Fitzjames, along with other relics and human remains on Beechey Island, King William Island, Nunavut, in Canada's Northwest Territories. The note detailed that the ships had become locked in the ice and abandoned, and that nine officers and fifteen crew, including Franklin, were dead. It also said the survivors planned to make for Back's Great Fish River on the Canadian mainland, on foot.

Contemporary scientific study suggests that the men died from hypothermia, scurvy, starvation and general exposure. They may also have suffered from lead poisoning. Some cut marks on their bones suggest cannibalism, so by all accounts it must have been hell on earth, and death was not easy.

In 2014, HMS *Erebus* was located at the bottom of Queen Maud Gulf, and HMS *Terror* was found in Terror Bay near King William Island. *Erebus* is in shallow water of only 11 metres, while *Terror* is at 24 metres, and in remarkable condition, largely due to the location and the cold water temperature.

Crozier has many geographical features named after him, including: Cape Crozier on Ross Island in Antarctica; Cape Crozier on King William Island in the Canadian Arctic; Crozier Strait, between Cornwallis and Bathurst Islands, also in the Canadian Arctic; Crozier Place, a street in Stanley, in the Falkland Islands; and Crozier Crater on the moon. A hydrographic survey vessel from 1919 also bore his name.

HMS *Erebus* and HMS *Terror* amid the ice.
A nineteenth-century engraving from *Le Tour du Monde*, 1860.

An 1856 portrait of Sir Robert McClure.

ROBERT MCCLURE

1807–1873

Robert McClure was an Irish polar explorer who was the first to transit the Northwest Passage, and to circumnavigate the Americas.

*

Robert John Le Mesurier McClure was born at The Rectory, North Main Street in Wexford town on 28 January 1807. His father was Captain Robert McClure, an officer with the 89th Regiment, Princess Victoria's Royal Irish Fusiliers, who met his mother, Jane Elgee, when he was stationed in Wexford. Captain McClure's regiment was known as 'Blayney's Bloodhounds', earning the name under the command of Lord Blayney for their relish in hunting down rebels during the 1798 Rebellion.

Robert's maternal grandfather was the Reverend John Elgee, a curate and later rector of St Iberius' Church of Ireland church in Wexford, which still exists. Robert's father was a first cousin of Jane Wilde, mother of Oscar Wilde. Captain McClure died five months before the birth of his son. When Robert reached the age of four, he was placed under the care of his godfather, General John Le Mesurier, Governor of Alderney in the Channel Islands, whose life had been saved in battle by McClure senior.

Robert entered Eton and later Sandhurst Military College, and in 1824, as a teenager, he joined the navy. The first ship on which he served was HMS *Victory*, and over the next twelve years, he served on different ships in far-flung parts of the world.

In 1836, Robert served on HMS *Terror* (the ship that would later be lost on the Franklin Expedition in 1845), under the command of Captain George Beck, bound for the North Pole. This gave Robert a taste of the hardships and dangers involved in Arctic exploration and first-hand experience of the treachery of huge ice floes.

He went to sea aboard HMS *Enterprise* in 1848, serving as First Lieutenant under Sir James Clark Ross, to find the lost Franklin Expedition (see pages 115–16).

Having failed to locate the expedition, *Enterprise* returned to Britain, and in 1850, McClure went on a new expedition, again to look for Franklin, this time from the west. Now Commander of HMS *Investigator*, McClure was accompanied by Richard Collinson as Commander of HMS *Enterprise*. The two ships sailed south through the Atlantic, navigating through the Straits of Magellan in Chile, to reach the Pacific Ocean.

The ships became separated at this point and had no further contact. *Investigator* turned north and crossed the Arctic Circle at the end of July 1850, via the Bering Strait. The weather had changed dramatically and in early August, the first ice floes were seen ahead, adorned with large herds of walruses. When they were close to shore, they sent a landing party, who erected a cairn of stones. They met local Inuit and gave them gifts of knives and mirrors, and much-loved tobacco. The ship's name was engraved on these items, so the next vessel travelling through would know they had been there.

The ship made good progress through the ice, passing Flaxman Island off the northern coast of Alaska on 18 August, and continuing north; however, shortly after this, larger ice floes became more plentiful, many up to ten to twelve kilometres long. Afraid his ship would be crushed, McClure headed south and at the end of August, they reached Cape Bathurst, the most northerly point of the Northwest Territories, where they saw pods of whales.

In early September, the ice floes increased in number and began to close in around the ship. She was thrown onto her starboard side and raised over half a metre out of the water with ice pressed in around the keel. *Investigator* was now well and truly locked in the ice and frozen in for the winter.

On 21 October 1850, Captain McClure and a crew of six set out by sledge for Barrow Strait, to the north of Banks

Island, leaving Lieutenant Haswell in command of the ship. The sledge overturned often and became very damaged on the journey. McClure sent one of his party, Mr Court, back for another sledge. Although conditions were unimaginably demanding and hazardous, McClure and his crew persevered.

During the winter, McClure went overland across Banks Island to a high vantage point on the north coast. It was here that the Northwest Passage was discovered, as McClure's party could clearly see Melville Island and the frozen waters of Melville Sound reached by the explorer William Parry on his westward journey in 1819.

McClure decided to attempt a navigation of the Passage when the ice melted, but he never succeeded. In the summer of 1851, Prince of Wales Strait, a part of the passage on the route east, was still blocked to the north by ice, so he turned back, hoping to navigate around Banks Island. He reached the Bay of Mercy, which he named for the refuge it provided. During this time, a sledge party made it to Melville Island and back, leaving a message, carved into a large rock, in Winter Harbour. By the spring of 1852, the crew were malnourished and exhausted. Help arrived from Lieutenant Bedford Pim, who walked for twenty-eight days over the ice to the *Investigator*. He had come from the *Resolute*, which had sailed from the east, or Atlantic, side and found the message left at Winter Harbour.

McClure was keen to sail the *Investigator* back to England, but had to abandon her. He and his crew then spent the winter of 1853 in the Arctic, where the *Resolute* became trapped in ice. In April 1854, McClure went east by sledge to Beechey Island, where he joined the *North Star*, taking him back to England. As was common practice at the time, when a captain returned without his ship, he was court martialled for its loss. However, McClure received an honourable acquittal. He was awarded £10,000 to share with his men and was knighted. He also received honours from the British and French Geographical Societies.

McClure later went on to serve in the Far East, in the Second China War of 1857 to 1860, where he commanded a division of the Naval Brigade before Canton, now Guangzhou, China, in 1858, earning the Order of the Bath. He eventually earned the rank of Vice Admiral in 1873, the year of his death. Many geographical features have been named after him: McClure Strait, McClure Bay and Cape McClure on the edge of the Canadian Northwest Territories, as well as the McClure Crater in the Mare Fecunditatis on the moon. He was survived by his wife, Ada Tudor, whom he married in 1869. He is buried in Kensal Green Cemetery, where his close relative Lady Jane Wilde is also buried.

HMS *Investigator* was found in 2010 off Banks Island in the Beaufort Sea.

Frank Hurley and Ernest Shackleton in front of their tent on the drifting ice floe called 'Patience Camp' in 1916. Between them is the stove on which all the cooking was done, the fuel being blubber and penguin skins.

ERNEST
SHACKLETON

1874–1922

Ernest Shackleton was an Irish explorer who led three expeditions to the Antarctic during the golden age of polar exploration.

*

Sir Ernest Henry Shackleton was born in Kilkea, County Kildare, on 15 February 1874, into a family of Quakers. He had nine siblings: his brother Frank and eight sisters. (Frank was notoriously a suspect in the theft of the Irish Crown Jewels, but was exonerated.)

Shackleton's father, Henry, moved the family to Sydenham, outside London, in 1884, after completing his medical studies. This was partly for better work opportunities but also because Irish nationalism was on the rise, and an Anglo-Irish family could be subjected to unwanted attention. Growing up in a house of women, Ernest was petted and adored. He regaled his sisters with madcap tales and was a voracious reader. Stories of empire and adventure sparked his interest in exploration. He attended Dulwich College from the age of thirteen, but was bored and often restless.

At sixteen, Shackleton expressed a desire to go to sea. His father agreed – reluctantly – and bought him a berth on *Hoghton Tower*, a square-rigged sailing ship. Even though he was from a middle-class background, Shackleton learned to mix with everyone, from the officers to the roughest of men. Initially teased and feeling out of place, through his storytelling and appetite for hard work, he earned the respect of his crewmates. His ability to charm anyone would serve him well all his life.

When he was just twenty-four, in 1898, Shackleton qualified as a master mariner, which meant he could command a British ship anywhere in the world. He heard about Robert Scott's plans for an expedition to Antarctica and applied. Though the two men publicly showed great respect towards each other, it has been suggested that there was animosity between them. Scott dismissed Shackleton's application, apparently because he was not from a Royal Navy background. However, in 1900, Shackleton got himself recommended, through the father of a friend, to Sir Clements Markham, president of the Royal Geographical Society and in charge of Scott's expedition, and was appointed third officer on the ship *Discovery*. In June, he was drafted into the Royal Navy Reserve with the rank of sub-lieutenant. His popularity with the officers and crew may also have irked Scott.

The *Discovery* Expedition was being sent to the Antarctic in a scientific and geographic capacity. Scott, a stickler for rules and regulations, insisted on running *Discovery* like a Royal Navy vessel. Shackleton was used to the less formal approach of the merchant navy.

The ship left London on 31 July 1901, arriving at the Antarctic coast on 9 January 1902. Shackleton took part in the first sledging expedition with scientists Edward A. Wilson and Hartley A. Ferrar from McMurdo Sound. *Discovery* overwintered in the ice. During this time, Shackleton edited the expedition newspaper, *The South Polar Times*, to keep everyone entertained.

In spite of their rivalry, when Scott initiated a march towards the South Pole, he brought Shackleton with him. They reached a record distance south of 82 degrees 17 minutes, beating the record set by James Clarke Ross in 1842.

The march introduced Shackleton to the perils of one of the most inhospitable environments on earth. All twenty-two sledge dogs died. The crew suffered frostbite, snow-blindness and scurvy. Shackleton himself fell ill, and when they returned to *Discovery*, Scott sent him home on the relief ship *Morning*. It has been suggested that Shackleton never forgave Scott for this slight. Another Irishman who served on this expedition was Tom Crean (see pages 135–40).

Once he recuperated, Shackleton returned to England and

eventually took up a post as secretary of the Royal Scottish Geographical Society. He married Emily Dorman and they had three children. Shackleton had a brief and unsuccessful stint in politics, and worked for the Scottish industrialist William Beardmore, but at the back of his mind throughout was another trip to Antarctica. He began the tedious work of securing financial backing, with help from Beardmore, which led to other investors.

On 7 August 1907, *Nimrod* left England for the South Pole as the British Antarctic Expedition and arrived at the eastern section of the Great Ice Barrier on 21 January 1908. Shackleton chose this side rather than McMurdo Sound to the west, as Scott felt he had ownership of it. However, the ice was incredibly unstable, which gave Shackleton no choice but to head for McMurdo Sound. After delays by weather, they made camp at Cape Royds. Shackleton and three others, including Frank Wild, who would join him on the Imperial Trans-Antarctic Expedition (1914–17), set off on a march south, and broke Scott's previous record by reaching 88 degrees 23 minutes south, only 112 miles from the South Pole. The return journey on thinning rations was hazardous, but they all made it back.

Other successes of the expedition included the first ascent of Mount Erebus, and discovering the approximate location of the magnetic South Pole on 16 January 1909. Shackleton was hugely feted on his return to England and published an account of the exploration.

Now a polar hero, Shackleton's honours included being made a Commander of the Royal Victorian Order, being awarded a knighthood and receiving a gold medal from the Royal Geographical Society. Each member of the expedition received a Polar Medal from the King. In his homeland, the Dublin papers also recognised Shackleton's feat.

Shackleton embarked on a busy lecture series, which helped pay off some of the debt he had amassed. Meanwhile, Scott's *Terra Nova* Expedition left in 1910, arriving at the South Pole on 17 January 1912, to find that Norwegian Roald Amundsen had beaten them by thirty-four days. None of the Scott's party returned alive.

Declaring himself no good at anything other than being an explorer, Shackleton made preparations for the Imperial Trans-Antarctic Expedition. Its purpose was to be the first to traverse the whole Antarctic continent.

Shackleton scrambled to raise funds and a crew of fifty-six, split equally among two ships: *Endurance*, which would take the main party to Vahsel Bay in the Weddell Sea, where six of them, led by Shackleton, would start to cross the continent; and *Aurora,* under Captain Aeneas Macintosh, with a supporting crew who would go to McMurdo Sound on the opposite side of Antarctica. The *Aurora* crew would lay supply depots along the Great Ice Barrier (Ross Ice Shelf), allowing Shackleton to complete his journey of almost 3,000 kilometres across the continent. Despite the outbreak of the First World War, *Endurance* left England on 8 August 1914, having received approval to proceed from Winston Churchill, First Lord of the Admiralty.

Endurance left Grytviken on South Georgia for the Weddell Sea on 5 December 1914. There was more ice than expected and by 19 January 1915, *Endurance* had become trapped. Nine months later, on 24 October, the hull was breached. Shackleton gave the order to abandon ship. On 21 November 1915, *Endurance*, to the sound of splintering timbers and groaning ice, slipped below the surface. It must have been an incredible, heart-wrenching moment.

They set up a camp on a large ice floe, hoping to drift to Paulet Island where stores lay, over 400 kilometres away. By 17 March, they were within ninety-seven kilometres of their goal, but the ice was impassable. The ice floe their camp was on then broke in two, and Shackleton ordered the crew into the three lifeboats: *Stancomb Wills*, *Dudley Docker* and *James Caird* (named for three of the expedition's sponsors). After five days on horrendous seas, they landed at Elephant Island. The island was inhospitable and far from shipping routes. The men were exhausted, and Shackleton was deeply concerned for their well-being.

Shackleton decided to make for the whaling station on South Georgia in *James Caird*, leaving the majority of the crew behind. With him were Frank Worsley, Harry McNish, John Vincent, Tom Crean and Timothy McCarthy (an Irishman from Kinsale, County Cork). It was a brave call, given the slim odds of survival.

For fifteen days, *James Caird* sailed through the often-violent Southern Ocean. Thanks to navigator Worsley, they finally saw the cliffs of South Georgia, but hurricane-strength winds made landing impossible. When they eventually reached shore, they were tired, hungry and exhausted. The whaling station was on the other side of the island, and Shackleton decided to cross the uncharted mountain terrain on foot. McNish, Vincent and McCarthy were left at the landing point as they were not able for the arduous journey ahead.

Shackleton, Worsley and Crean, taking the clothes they stood up in, some rope and a carpenter's adze, set out. They put nails into the soles of their boots for grip on the ice. They travelled over fifty kilometres of unknown and treacherous terrain in difficult weather. Eventually, exhausted and starving, they arrived at the whaling station at Stromness on 20 May 1916. It was an unimaginable feat of bravery.

Shackleton's first three attempts to reach the crew on Elephant Island were foiled by ice, but the fourth was successful. After four and a half months, all twenty-two men were rescued.

The *Aurora* also ran into trouble and had to return to New Zealand. They succeeded in their mission of laying depots, but lost three men, including Captain Mackintosh.

When Shackleton and his crew returned home, Britain was in the grip of the First World War. After various appointments through the war years, Shackleton decided on one last expedition to the Antarctic in 1921. However, he took ill in Rio de Janeiro on 16 September 1921. Refusing a proper medical examination, he pushed on to South Georgia where, on 5 January 1922, he suffered a heart attack and died. On hearing of her husband's death, Emily asked that he be buried in South Georgia. He was laid to rest in Grytviken. One hundred years after he was buried, on 5 March 2022, *Endurance* was found by the ice breaker SA *Agulhas II*, over three kilometres deep in the Weddell Sea.

Shackleton's death marked the end of the Heroic Age of polar exploration. He was one of a breed of men whose insatiable thirst for adventure and enormous courage expanded our knowledge of our planet. His name will be forever remembered for the determination, courage and no small amount of madness he displayed in the face of incredible adversity.

Frank Hurley's iconic image of *Endurance* trapped in the ice.

Tom Crean pictured on the *Terra Nova* expedition of 1910–13.

TOM CREAN
1877–1938

Probably the first name that comes to mind when thinking of the Irish and polar exploration is Tom Crean. This is largely thanks to Michael Smith's biography *An Unsung Hero*, published in 2000. Prior to this, Crean's name was almost lost to history, despite having taken part in three of the most important Antarctic expeditions.

*

Crean was born near Annascaul on the Dingle Peninsula, County Kerry, in February 1877, one of eleven children. He left school at twelve to help out on the family farm. The wild Atlantic waves surrounding the Dingle Peninsula must have struck a young boy with a thirst for adventure, looking to escape the hardships of working the land. The Great Hunger was still in the public memory, and the threat of eviction was all too prevalent. The tough conditions of his childhood would stand to him throughout his life.

Several of Crean's brothers emigrated and there was a tradition in the area, as in many rural Irish places, of sons joining the Royal Navy. It promised travel and excitement and a life of adventure. Tom enlisted on 10 July 1893, when he was not quite sixteen.

Crean's apprenticeship began aboard the training ship HMS *Impregnable*. He worked aboard various other vessels and managed to see a bit of the world. On HMS *Wild Swan*, he went to South America, where the ship joined the Pacific Station. He also made his way up the ranks and became an able seaman. In 1900, he served aboard *Ringarooma*, a cruiser in the Royal Navy's Australian squadron. *Ringarooma* was ordered to assist Captain Robert Scott's *Discovery* when she was docked at Lyttelton Harbour, New Zealand, awaiting supplies before heading south on the British National Antarctic Expedition. After an able seaman absconded following an incident with a petty officer, Crean volunteered to replace him, and thus his career as a polar explorer began.

Discovery made her way south, and in little over a month arrived at McMurdo Sound, on 8 February 1902. They set up a base at a spot later called Hut Point, from which they made sledging expeditions. The strong Kerry man soon proved to be adept at hauling sledges. His pleasant countenance and good humour endeared him to his comrades. Even in punishing conditions, he was able to keep smiling.

Crean took part in three major sledging trips across the Great Ice Shelf to lay supply depots. Scott would rely on these when he took the journey south, along with Ernest Shackleton and Edward Wilson. In 1902, *Discovery* became locked in the ice and Crean was one of those who stayed until she was freed, in February 1904. Conditions must have been harsh over the Antarctic winter, but Scott, clearly impressed with Crean, promoted him to petty officer, first class.

After returning to Britain, Crean served aboard a number of vessels, including some that were under Scott's command. When it came to Scott's second expedition – the British Antarctic Expedition on *Terra Nova* – with the aim this time of finding the South Pole and securing its discovery for Britain, amongst the first he recruited was the Kerry man. Crean had proved himself to be a resilient and reliable character.

The *Terra Nova* Expedition arrived in McMurdo Sound in January 1911, having left Britain in June 1910. Crean was one of the men who built One Ton Depot, a huge supply depot on the route to the Pole. On the way back to Cape Evans, Crean and two others almost lost their lives when camping on unstable ice. It broke up, leaving them isolated on a dangerous floe. It was Crean who went for help, leaping from ice floe to ice floe, and he ultimately saved their lives.

Crean left with Scott and others for an attempt on the Pole in November 1911. An arduous journey, it meant trekking 650 kilometres (400 miles) across the Great Ice Barrier; 200

kilometres (120 miles) over the Beardmore Glacier, which was 3,000 metres (10,000 feet) above sea level; and finally the mere matter of another 560 kilometres (350 miles) to the South Pole: a difficult and exhausting endeavour in normal weather, unimaginable in Antarctic conditions. Tom Crean was one of the group of eight who reached 87 degrees 32 minutes south, only 270 kilometres (168 miles) from the Pole. From here, five went on to the pole: Scott, Edgar Evans, Wilson, Bowers and Oates, all officers. Crean was bitterly disappointed at not being chosen, but in hindsight, it saved his life.

Crean's journey back was horrendous: the terrain was treacherous, and food supplies were low. One of the party, Lieutenant Evans, became severely ill, and showed signs of scurvy. Lashly and Crean hauled him along on a sledge. They reached Corner Camp on 18 February, some fifty-six kilometres (thirty-five miles) from Hut Point, at which stage it was decided that Crean alone should go for help. With a meagre three biscuits and two sticks of chocolate to keep him going, he made it just ahead of a severe blizzard. It was a phenomenal feat of heroism and endurance.

However, the party that went on to the South Pole never returned. In November 1912, Crean was one of the men who went out in a search party to find them, which they did on 12 November. Crean noted in a letter that, with Scott's death, he had 'lost a good friend'.

The remaining crew of *Terra Nova* returned to Britain and were awarded the Polar Medal by King George V. Crean and Lashly were also awarded the Albert Medal for saving Lieutenant Evans' life.

Only two years later, on 25 May 1914, Crean joined Ernest Shackleton on the Imperial Transantarctic Expedition, as second officer (see pages 129–32). His many duties included looking after the dogs: Shackleton had learned from Amundsen's success in his 1911 expedition to the Pole that dog sleds were more effective than man hauling. Shackleton already knew Crean from the *Discovery* Expedition and understood the sheer strength of character he possessed. There is no doubt that Shackleton recognised a little of himself in his fellow Irishman. When Shackleton set off on his last-ditch effort to save his crew by sailing across 800 miles of Southern Ocean from Elephant Island to South Georgia, Crean was one of the five he picked to accompany him. Crean was also one of the three who made the incredible journey across the uncharted mountains of South Georgia to reach help.

Crean returned to Britain in 1916, at the height of the First World War, and in 1917 married Eileen Herlihy. He retired from the Royal Navy in 1920 and settled in Annascaul, where he and Eileen raised a small family. He opened a pub, which is still there today: The South Pole Inn.

It was a difficult time politically in Ireland, and particularly in County Kerry, which was a stronghold of republican ideals. Crean's older brother Cornelius, who served in the Royal Irish Constabulary, was killed in an IRA ambush. Tom put away his three Polar Medals, and hardly ever spoke of his extraordinary journeys to the Antarctic.

Crean died in 1938, aged just sixty-one, when an infection developed after surgery for a burst appendix. He is buried in Annascaul.

His legacy includes a peak in Antarctica called Mount Crean; Crean Glacier and Crean Lake in South Georgia; and Mount Crean in Greenland. An Irish Marine research vessel, the RV *Tom Crean*, is named in his honour.

WORTHY

OF

NOTE

JAMES LEANDER CATHCART

1767–1843

Born in Mount Murragh, County Westmeath, in 1767, James Leander Cathcart was a sailor noted for his testimony of his time as a slave of Barbary pirates.

*

When he was eight, Cathcart emigrated to America with a group of colonists. His father placed him in the care of a relative, John Cathcart, a sea captain. He joined the American Revolution when he was twelve, serving on a private vessel. He was keen for adventure and, filled with patriotic zeal, wanted to serve his new country. At the age of fifteen, he was aboard *The Confederacy* as a midshipman. It taught him a great deal, as he learnt both sailing technique and Portuguese from the helmsman; and navigation, mathematics and Spanish from the navigator. *The Confederacy* was captured by the British and Cathcart spent three years on British prison ships. He eventually escaped and made his way back to America.

After the war, he decided on a merchant navy career. His love of the sea and knowledge of languages helped him in this endeavour. He enlisted as second mate on the *Maria Boston*, bound for Cadiz.

Whilst aboard the *Maria Boston* in 1785, he and twenty other sailors were taken prisoner by Barbary pirates and put into service as slaves. He spent eleven years as a slave in Algiers, enduring harsh conditions, including severe beatings. The prisoners went without food a great deal of the time and were often shackled in irons for long periods. They endured hard labour, and many died from plague. At the gate of the Dey's palace stood a square area where many prisoners were beheaded for any kind of crime.

English ships engage with Barbary corsairs, in a painting by Willem van de Velde the Younger, *c.* 1695.

Surviving all this through intelligence and wit, Cathcart managed to improve his situation considerably. He became fluent in Arabic and Turkish, and eventually became clerk of the prison he served in. He eventually became chief clerk to the Dey (the governor of Algeria). One of the jobs entrusted to Cathcart was feeding the Dey's pet lions; naturally, Cathcart kept the best cuts of meat, smuggling them through to his fellow prisoners.

Cathcart mediated between the Dey and Colonel David Humphreys, the US Minister to Portugal, resulting in the Treaty of Algiers of 1796. The treaty opened up shipping rights between the Barbary Coast and the US, and ultimately brought Cathcart his freedom. He had managed to raise funds to buy a tavern, and when he was freed, he bought a ship which he sailed to America, along with the surviving members of his original crew.

He married Jane Bancker Woodside on 5 June 1798 and lived for a time in Georgetown. He moved to Madeira in 1807 as Consul General, and for a time to Cadiz – the port he had been destined for as a young man before fate sent him elsewhere. He returned to Washington in 1817 and died there in 1843, having served as a diplomat for John Adams, Thomas Jefferson and James Madison. His daughter, J.B. Newkirk, published his story posthumously in 1899, based on his diaries, called *The Captive: Eleven Years a Prisoner in Algiers*.

KATE TYRRELL

1863–1921

Amongst Ireland's many maritime museums is the excellent Arklow Maritime and Heritage Museum. Tucked in a corner there is an account of an extraordinary and formidable woman, who was decades ahead of her time, and who through bravery and necessity helped to change the world for seafaring women.

*

The Tyrrell name and Arklow are synonymous with seafaring and shipping. Since the 1770s, generations of Tyrrells have owned, skippered or built boats in Arklow. Jack Tyrrell built the famous *Gypsy Moth III*, in which Francis Chichester won the first solo transatlantic yacht race in 1960. Jack also built the brigantine STV *Asgard II*, the Irish national sail-training vessel, in 1981, which sank in the Bay of Biscay in 2008.

Kate Tyrrell was born to Edward Tyrrell and his wife, Elizabeth, in 1863, the second of four daughters. Her father was a noted mariner and owned several schooners on which he sailed as master. He was also an astute and successful businessman.

Kate showed a fiery and abrupt personality from a young age, and this served her well in an Ireland that had just come through the Great Hunger. Even though her family were prosperous, she and her sisters were exposed to the psychological scars such an event leaves.

Their mother was very strict, and the four girls were always immaculately dressed going to school. Kate preferred to spend time with her father on his ships, however. From an early age, she was fascinated by navigational equipment and sea charts. By the time she was twelve, she could write up shipping journal entries and records. None of this took from her conventional education, in which she did very well, learning bookkeeping and business studies. Edward, having no sons, saw Kate as someone who could take over the family business.

In April 1882, Kate sailed to Connah's Quay in Wales with her father and his long-time associate Laurence Brennan. They returned to discover that her second-youngest sister, Alecia, was very ill with consumption, or tuberculosis. Alecia died in May, and her death affected Kate and her family terribly. Her mother became ill, and Kate had to take over the task of keeping books for her father's ships. Elizabeth deteriorated to such a degree that Edward stayed at home to look after her and left the running of his ships to Kate and Laurence Brennan. Elizabeth died from consumption on 12 December 1882. In 1885, the 22-year-old Kate became, in effect, a mother to her two sisters, Lucy and Ellen, and ran her father's business. Finding herself thrust into a position of enormous responsibility, she set about it with diligence.

In 1885, Edward decided to purchase a new schooner, the *Denbighshire Lass*, for Kate and her sisters. A 61-ton Liverpool schooner, she was twenty-two metres (seventy-two feet four inches) long. Like other schooners of the period, she could bear a lot of weight for her size, and could be sailed by as few as two or three people. It was simply unheard of at the time for a woman to be the registered owner of a ship, but Edward registered the schooner in Kate's name. They sailed the ship home to Dublin initially to register it, and then to Arklow, their home port. Even though Kate was a slight and small woman, by all accounts she handled the sailing brilliantly.

In 1885, the *Denbighshire Lass* had a very busy year. She was skippered by Laurence Brennan with a crew of three: a mate, an able seaman and a ship's boy. Edward also spent time aboard along with Kate, who sailed on her whenever she could. Her father, who had a long-term heart issue, worsened by the tragic events in his family life, died on 7 July 1886 at Garston, Liverpool, on board the *Denbighshire Lass*. Kate had to arrange for her father's remains to be brought home and buried. In a short space of time, she had lost her mother, sister and now her father, and was effectively head of the family and the business. She was also the managing owner of the ship.

However, as a woman, she could not be on much of the official shipping paperwork, she made the decision to have Laurence Brennan officially listed as the owner. It wasn't until 1914 that she herself became the official owner.

Despite the harrowing circumstances that Kate found herself in, the business thrived under her leadership. However, tragedy struck again, and on 17 November 1888, her youngest sister, Lucy, died of consumption, aged twenty. Kate and Ellen were now alone.

Kate threw herself into the business, dealing with the rules and regulations of ports and docks, and keeping meticulous records. She changed the rigging of the *Denbighshire Lass* from schooner to ketch in 1918 (a ketch's rigging is easier to look after, as it is reduced to a main mast and a mizzen. Both sails are forward of the rudder, but about the same height). She supervised the ship's repairs and could hold her own when talking with shipwrights. The ship mainly worked the route to Liverpool and her chief cargoes were coal, bricks and textiles, but she also sailed several Irish routes, from Arklow to Dungarvan, Waterford and Dublin. The ship also sailed to the Iberian peninsula, bringing back iron ore. When Ellen married, becoming Mrs Hyland, Kate received Ellen's share of the shipping business and became sole owner of the *Denbighshire Lass*.

Kate herself was contemplating wedlock and in 1896, she married John Fitzpatrick, nephew of Laurence Brennan.

With John as master and Kate as the owner, they made a formidable team. However, she insisted on keeping her own name. She bore a son, James, in 1900, and a daughter, Elizabeth, in 1905, which was a difficult birth.

During the First World War (1914–18), shipping was dangerous and difficult, although highly profitable. German U-boats were capable of targeting any craft flying the Red Ensign of the British Crown, as all Irish ships had to do.

Politically, Ireland was in turmoil. The 1916 Rising led to a period of huge unrest in the country. Kate's last surviving sister, Ellen, also died in 1916.

The Kynoch munitions factory had been established in Arklow in 1896, bringing a lot of shipping to the port, as it supplied arms to the British military, in particular for the Boer War and the First World War. Kynock's closed in 1918, after an explosion in 1917 that killed twenty-seven people. This was a large blow to the town and had an effect on the local shipping industry too. However, Kate and John Fitzpatrick continued to trade.

Now in her fifties, Kate was no longer quite the force she had once been. It was mostly her husband, John, and son James who sailed the *Denbighshire Lass*. In 1921, Kate ensured an Irish tricolour was kept in the skipper's cabin, to be used once it was safe to do so. Her health deteriorated until she was more or less housebound, with her daughter looking after her.

She died peacefully at home on 4 October 1921.

John and James continued to sail the *Denbighshire Lass*, and in the 1920s made many voyages to Cardiff and Swansea. On one voyage to Swansea, the ship sailed the Irish tricolour, the first vessel to do so in a British port. It caused quite a stir! Few of the other ships in port – Italian, Russian and British – knew what it was.

Eventually, Kate's daughter, Elizabeth, on the death of her father, sold the *Denbighshire Lass* to a British buyer. On 16 March 1926, she sailed the Bristol Channel, and sprang a leak near The Smalls. The weather turned for the worst, and the crew abandoned ship. She foundered and met a watery grave there.

Through insurmountable loss, Kate Tyrrell had not only survived but thrived. Through necessity, she stood firm in a male-dominated society and workplace, and is remembered as an extraordinary lady mariner.

The *Denbighshire Lass* painted by Rueban Chappelle (1870–1940).

CONOR O'BRIEN

1880–1952

Conor O'Brien was the second amateur sailor to circumnavigate the globe and the first to do so under the Irish tricolour.

*

Edward Conor Marshall O'Brien was born in London on 3 November 1880, to a family with very strong Irish connections. His grandfather, William Smith O'Brien, was a leader of the Young Irelanders, which was both a political and cultural movement committed to the Irish struggle for independence, founded in 1842. William also served as an MP for Ennis. Although a member of a prominent, ascendency Protestant family, he believed in Catholic emancipation and had a love for the Irish language. This heritage influenced Conor, who also spoke Irish and was a member of Sinn Féin. Conor received his education in England at Winchester College and Oxford, and also at Trinity College Dublin.

O'Brien lived in Dublin for a time and worked as an architect. He designed two public buildings, the Co-operative Hall in Donegal and the People's Hall in Limerick. He also

The *Ilen* moored at Baltimore Harbour, west Cork.

designed two ships, the *Saoirse* and the *Ilen*, both of which he captained.

In July 1914, the Howth gun-running saw 1,500 rifles smuggled into Ireland for the Irish Volunteers. The guns had been purchased in Germany by Sir Roger Casement, Erskine Childers and Darrell Figgis. Childers' yacht *Asgard* and O'Brien's yacht *Kelpie* sailed to a buoy near the Belgian coast, where they met a tugboat from Hamburg that carried the guns. The boats were stuffed with arms, leaving very little room for sleeping or dining. The journey back to Ireland was not without incident, as they fell foul of bad weather and encountered a British naval fleet, but they survived both. The arms on *Kelpie* were transferred to the yacht *Chotah*, before being brought ashore in Kilcoole, Wicklow, in August 1914. A fascinating historical aside is that the mission, involving the *Asgard*, *Kelpie* and *Chotah*, was exclusively planned, funded and executed by aristocratic members of the Protestant Anglo-Irish Ascendancy. It was financed by Alice Stopford Green, who lived in London and was a granddaughter of the Protestant Archbishop of Meath. The plan was hatched in her London home with Casement.

After this mission, O'Brien served in the Royal Naval Volunteer Reserve, a volunteer force of the Royal Navy, during the First World War. He joined to gain a solid grounding in navigation.

In 1923, in *Saoirse*, he left Foynes port in Limerick, along with three crew, and took to the sea to sail around the world via the Cape of Good Hope (southern Africa), Cape Leeuwin (southwestern Australia) and Cape Horn (the southernmost point of South America).

Unlike many of the large vessels that took the so-called clipper route, *Saoirse* was only a thirteen-metre-long vessel, so it was quite the feat. The clipper route to Australia saw vessels run from west to east via the Cape of Good Hope and the Southern Ocean. This way they made best use of the infamous westerly and southerly winds known as the Roaring Forties, notoriously strong and dangerous. Clippers were mid-nineteenth-century ships built for speed. They were narrow for their length and carried a huge amount of sail, to take advantage of these boiling seas. Clippers were typically about seventy metres long (the famous *Cutty Sark* is sixty-five metres long), five times the size of the *Saoirse*.

O'Brien's remarkable journey gave him and *Saoirse* a number of firsts: he became the first Irish yachtsman to circumnavigate the globe, *Saoirse* the first small boat to do it via the three Great Capes and the first to enter ports along the way with the new tricolour of Ireland. O'Brien returned to Dún Laoghaire to great fanfare in June 1925. He documented his journey in a book called *Across Three Oceans*. Published in 1927, it is still in print.

During his epic voyage aboard *Saoirse*, O'Brien stopped off at the Falkland Islands in 1924. While he was there, the Falklands Island Company asked him to design and build a vessel, which later became *Ilen*, named for a river near Baltimore in County Cork. It was used as a Falklands Island service boat, and O'Brien sailed it there himself. He arrived in January 1927. The *Ilen* returned to Baltimore in 1998 and, after a full restoration, was relaunched in 2018.

On 10 October 1928, O'Brien married Kitty Clausen, an English painter. He was forty-seven and she was six years his junior. Kitty sailed with him on *Saoirse*, her seamanship earning O'Brien's admiration.

O'Brien wrote several more books, including *Voyage and Discovery*, which was illustrated by Kitty. It was the first English-language travel book about Ibiza, and was published in 1933. Kitty died in 1936 at the age of fifty.

O'Brien was an avid outdoor enthusiast: he climbed Mount Brandon in Kerry barefoot and Mount Snowdon in Wales with George Mallory, a climber who took part in the first three British expeditions to attempt an ascent of Mount Everest. O'Brien sold his beloved *Saoirse* in 1936 and retired to Foynes Island, where he died in 1952. He published fourteen books during his lifetime, including six children's books. *Saoirse* foundered in 1979 while at anchor during a hurricane, but a replica has recently been built by Liam Hegarty in Cork.

Gottfried von Banfield on the cover of a supplement in the *Linzer Tages Post* in 1917.

GOTTFRIED VON BANFIELD

1890–1986

Known as 'The Eagle of Trieste', Gottfried Freiherr von Banfield was one of the most successful Austro-Hungarian naval aeroplane pilots of the First World War. He was one of the few flying aces of the war, scoring at least nine aerial victories over the Adriatic Sea.

*

The Banfields, of Norman origin, were a Quaker merchant family from Clonmel, County Tipperary. Gottfried's grandfather Thomas Collins Banfield was born in Bandon, County Cork, and worked as an accountant for the British Army. Thomas married Josephine von Frech, an Austrian aristocrat, in Vienna in 1853; he later died in the Crimean War after the taking of Sevastopol. His son Richard was an Austro-Hungarian citizen. A gunnery officer with the Austro-Hungarian Navy, he served as a commander on the *Erherzhog Ferdinand Max* (a broadside ironclad, the flagship of the Austro-Hungarian Navy in the 1860s) during the Battle of Lissa in 1886, a battle with Italy.

Richard's brother Alfred also served in the same navy.

Richard's son Gottfried was born in Castelnuovo, Montenegro, in 1890. He attended naval school in Fiume, from where he emerged as a cadet in 1909. A mere three years later, in 1912, he was promoted to frigate-lieutenant. Later that year, he obtained his flying licence from the flying school in Wiener Neustadt. He was one of the first pilots in the Austro-Hungarian Navy and he perfected his skills under Jean-Louis Conneau, a famous pilot of the time, known as Beaumont. Part of his training involved working with seaplanes.

With war looming, von Banfield's flying prowess was put to great use, and made him a hero for the Austro-Hungarians. He started out on a flying boat for battleship SMS *Zrínyi* as part of a reconnaissance mission and saw action against Montenegro in the air. When the Italians entered the war, he was commissioned to build a seaplane station near Trieste, and was the commanding officer, a post he held until the end of the war in 1918. He won air battles against the French and Italians in a Lohner biplane in the Gulf of Trieste in 1915. The Lohner L biplane was the highest technology of the day, but by contemporary standards it appears flimsy and exposed. It was a two-bay biplane, with the engine mounted on struts in the gap between both wings, flown solo.

In 1916, von Banfield flew a monoplane, and won many victories, finding his place amongst the flying aces of the day. Later that year, he developed a fighter aircraft, which had a machine gun bolted to the hull in front of the cockpit. He shot an Allied flying boat on 31 May 1917, and became the first Austro-Hungarian pilot to down an enemy aircraft at night. He was wounded in 1918, but survived the war, the most decorated pilot of the Empire.

Von Banfield was awarded the Grand Military Merit Medal with Swords for his war service in 1916, an honour normally reserved for those of high rank such as generals. In August 1917, he received the Military Order of Maria Theresa, thus receiving the title of 'Freiherr' or baron, and adding it to his family name. At the time of his death in 1986, he was the last living Knight of the Military Order of Maria Theresa.

When Trieste came under Italian rule after the war, von Banfield was imprisoned for a time, but in 1920, he emigrated to Britain along with his wife, Contessa Maria Tripcovich of Trieste, and became a British subject. They lived in Newcastle upon Tyne. In 1926, von Banfield returned to Trieste and became director of the Diodato Tripcovich and Co. Trieste Shipping Company, taking over from his father-in-law. He was known in the city as *Il nostro Barone* or 'Our Baron'. He was also invited to give a lecture to the Military History Society of Ireland in 1965.

Von Banfield was the honorary Consul of France at Trieste and received the French Legion of Honour in 1977. He died at the great age of ninety-six on 23 September 1986 in Trieste.

Gottfried von Banfield (right) at the airbase in Trieste c.1917, with the Lohner L flying boat behind him.

REFERENCES

Brendan of Clonfert

de Courcy Ireland, John, *Ireland and the Irish in Maritime History.*
Gandale Press, 1986.

Simms, George Otto, *Brendan the Navigator: Exploring the Ancient World.*
The O'Brien Press, 1989.

Wallace, Martin, *Celtic Saints: Pocket Guide.* Appletree Press, 2007.

John Barry

Fowler, Jr., William M., *Rebels Under Sail: The American Navy during the
Revolution.* Scribner, 1976.

McGrath, Tim, *John Barry: An American Hero in the Age of Sail.*
Westholme Publishing, 2010.

Williams, Thomas, *America's First Flag Officer: Father of the American
Navy.* AuthorHouse, 2008.

ushistory.org, accessed 12 March 2025.

William Brown

admiralbrown.com, accessed 18 April 2024.

de Courcy Ireland, John, *The Admiral from Mayo: A Life of Almirante
William Brown of Foxford, Father of the Argentine Navy.* Edmund
Burke Publisher, 1995.

irishships.com/famous_irish_mariners.html#Brown by Brian Vale,
accessed 18 April 2024.

mariner.ie/admiral-william-brown/, accessed 18 April 2024.

Peter Campbell

Coogan, Tim Pat, *Wherever Green is Worn – The Story of the Irish Diaspora.*
Arrow Books, 2002.

Irish Migration Studies in Latin America Vol. 4 No 1 January–February
2006.

irlandes.org, accessed 20 April 2024.

irishships.com/famous_irish_mariners.html#Campbell by Brian Vale, accessed 20 April 2024.

Bartholemew Hayden

irishships.com/famous_irish_mariners.html#BartholomewHayden by Brian Vale, accessed 21 April 2024.

Thomas Charles Wright

irlandeses.org/dilab_wrightt.htm, accessed 20 April 2024.

independent.ie/regionals/louth/drogheda-news/thomas-wright-is-honoured/37122392.html, accessed 20 April 2024.

theirishatwar.com/2020/01/26/father-of-ecuadorian-navy-thomas-charles-wright-born-in-drogheda-1799/, accessed 20 April 2024.

Wilcox, Martin, '"These Peaceable Times are the Devil": Royal Navy Officers in the Post-War Slump, 1815–1825', *International Journal of Maritime History*. July 2014.

Robert Halpin

Maritime Museum of Ireland, Halpin biography information board.

Rees, Jim, *The Life of Captain Robert Halpin*. Dee-Jay Publications, 1992.

John de Robeck

dib.ie/biography/de-robeck-sir-john-michael-a2469, accessed 11 May 2024.

britannica.com/event/Naval-Operations-in-the-Dardanelles-Campaign-1915#ref1245311, accessed 11 May 2024.

Andrew Cunningham

britannica.com/biography/Andrew-Browne-Cunningham, accessed 12 May 2024.

Simpson, Michael, 'Cunningham, Andrew Browne, Viscount Cunningham of Hyndhope (1883–1963)', *Oxford Dictionary of National Biography*. 2011.

James Forrestal

britannica.com/biography/James-V-Forrestal, accessed 12 May 2024.

forrestalhistory.com/the-forrestal-kennedy-connection/, accessed 12 May
    2024.
history.navy.mil/content/history/nhhc/browse-by-topic/people/sec-nav/
    forrestal/james-forrestal.html, accessed 18 May 2024.
washingtonpost.com/archive/lifestyle/1999/05/23/the-fall-of-james-
    forrestal/60c653b3-c537-462f-b523-5fdc5cd934aa/, accessed 18 May
    2024.

Francis Beaufort

Hare, David, *The Great Lighthouses of Ireland*. Gill Books, 2022.
Chart 5011 (Edition 4) Symbols and Abbreviations used on Admiralty
    Paper Charts, Office of the Admiralty, 2004.
de Courcy Ireland, John, 'Francis Beaufort: Wind Scale'. On-line
    Journal of Research on Irish Maritime History, accessed 19 May
    2024.

John Holland

britannica.com/biography/John-Philip-Holland, accessed 1 June 2024.
dib.ie/biography/holland-john-philip-a4063, accessed 1 June 2024.
Morris, Richard Knowles, *John P. Holland, 1841–1914: Inventor of the
    Modern Submarine.* University of South Carolina Press, 1998.
web.archive.org/web/20200813112758/https://johnpholland.ie/
    documentary/, accessed 1 June 2024.

Maude Delap and Annie Massey

Finn, Clodagh, 'Maude Delap: the pioneering marine biologist who broke
    bias in her field'. *Irish Examiner*, 7 March 2022.
Webb, Sarah, Blazing a Trail: Irish Women Who Changed the World. The
    O'Brien Press, 2018.

Granuaile

Chambers, Anne, *Grace O'Malley: The Biography of Ireland's Pirate Queen,
    1530–1603.* Gill Books, 2019.
Ekin, Des, *Ireland's Pirate Trail: A Quest to Uncover Our Swashbuckling
    Past.* The O'Brien Press, 2021.

Anne Bonny

annebonnypirate.com/, accessed 22 June 2024.

Ekin, Des, *Ireland's Pirate Trail: A Quest to Uncover Our Swashbuckling Past.* The O'Brien Press, 2021.

Francis Crozier

Smith, Michael, *Icebound in the Arctic: The Mystery of Captain Francis Crozier and the Franklin Expedition.* The O'Brien Press, 2021.

Robert McClure

Gaul, Liam, *Famous Wexfordians.* The History Press of Ireland, 2019.

Kiely, Des, *Famous Wexford People in History.* Parsifal Press, 2018.

Laughton, J.K., 'McClure, Sir Robert John le Mesurier (1807–1873)'. Oxford Dictionary of National Biography, 2004.

Ernest Shackleton

Bound, Mensun, *The Ship Beneath the Ice: The Discovery of Shackleton's Endurance*. Pan, 2023.

Fiennes, Ranulph, *Shackleton: A Biography*. Michael Joseph, 2021.

Smith, Michael, *Shackleton: By Endurance We Conquer.* The Collins Press, 2015.

Tom Crean

Smith, Michael, *An Unsung Hero: Tom Crean – Antarctic Survivor.* The Collins Press, 2000.

James Leander Cathcart

archive.org/details/captives00cathrich/page/n23/mode/2up?view=theater

commonplace.online/article/the-greatest-eloquence/, accessed 15 June 2024.

Kate Tyrrell

Forde, Frank, *Maritime Arklow.* The Glendale Press, 1988.

Mahon, John, *Kate Tyrrell 'Lady Mariner': The Story of the extraordinary woman who sailed the* Denbighshire Lass. Basement Press, 1995.

Conor O'Brien

afloat.ie/sail/offshore/solo-sailing/conor-o-brien/item/62159-another-first-for-conor-o-brien-his-alternative-image-of-an-unknown-ibiza, accessed 16 June 2024.

Hall, Judith, *In Search of Islands*. The Collins Press, 2009.

O'Brien, Conor, *Across Three Oceans: A Voyage in the Yacht Saoirse*. Independently published, 2023.

the-emigre.com/column/the-forgotten-irishman, accessed 16 June 2024.

Gottfried von Banfield

Chant, Christopher. *Austro-Hungarian Aces of World War 1.* Osprey Publishing, 2002.

McNally, Frank, 'The Wild Goose who flew like an Eagle – An Irishman's Diary about Gottfried Freiherr von Banfield', *The Irish Times*, accessed 17 March 2025.

museum.ie/en-IE/Collections-Research/Art-and-Industry-Collections/Art-Industry-Collections-List/Military-History/Irish-soldiers-at-home,-abroad,-and-in-the-21st-Ce/Soldiering-Abroad, accessed 14 March 2025.

O'Connor, Martin, *Air Aces of the Austro-Hungarian Empire 1914-1918.* Flying Machine Press, 1994.

thejournal.ie/world-war-one-irish-characters-1803640-Nov2014/, accessed 29 June 2024.

PHOTOGRAPH CREDITS

The author and publisher thank the following for permission to use illustrative material: Shutterstock: background map and decorative graphic elements used throughout, also photo on p. 18; Jonathan Rossney: p. 2; Alamy: pp 25, 28, 42, 46, 56, 62, 67, 68, 73, 74, 82, 85, 88, 100, 106, 117, 118, 124, 133, 134, 144, 154; author's collection: 35, 146, 152; Wikimedia Commons: pp 36, 41 (top and bottom), 50, 112, 142, 158, 162; Bernard Picton: p. 95.

Every effort has been made to trace copyright holders and to obtain their permission for the use of copyright material. The publisher apologises for any errors or omissions and would be grateful if notified of any corrections that should be incorporated in future reprints or editions of this book.

BEAUFORT NUMBER	WIND SPEED (MPH)
0	Under 1
1	1–3
2	4–7
3	8–12
4	13–18
5	19–24
6	25–31
7	32–38
8	39–46
9	47–54
10	55–63
11	64–72
12	73 or higher

B E A U F O R T   W I N D   S C A L E